# River of a Thousand Tales

## Encounters with Spirit, Reflections from Science

RAO KOLLURU

PARAVIEW PRESS

NEW YORK

*These tales are dedicated to*
*the infinite Self that dwells within us all.*

# Contents

# Foreword

You are about to embark on a pilgrimage to the east and to the west, outward and inward, and beyond. In our journey together, we will be discovering the mundane and the sublime, mind and matter, the finite and the infinite.

This book is a result of many forces, a few known, the other mostly unknown and perhaps unknowable. It embodies my own search for I knew not what. I wandered into mountains and valleys, and journeyed to Ashrams and sages and savants to reveal to me whatever it was I had been impelled to seek.

My quest began many years ago. I don't know when the seed was planted, but I do remember when I first started to ponder Karma. It was at a time when I had just finished writing another book on environment and health. It was a time of fundamental shifts, of travels and travails, a time of reflection. The result is this book and an earlier companion, In Quest of the Infinite.

Over the years, my odyssey brought me to sages and holy places—in and out of churches, temples and shrines in the West and the East, Up and Down—in America, India, Japan, China, and elsewhere. It was in the Himalayas that I first made my cosmic connection. It seemed only natural that those lofty precincts inspired so much of science and spirit so long ago—from zero to infinity, from yoga to chess, from karate to kamasutra.

In March 1997, I was trekking the banks of the river Ganges at the Himalayan foothills in search of ancient wisdom. I came face to face with a *Rishi* and was drawn at once into an illuminating discourse. Then I asked his name. I felt awkward in doing so but wanted to acknowledge his contribution to the book. He said with a chuckle—overlooking my western mannerisms—that his kindred spirits had no possessions, not even names, and didn't need them. Of such were the original wellsprings of these insights. He, along with so many others, must therefore remain nameless. But their spirit is here with us.

This book is about many things. It's about human nature. It's about duties and rewards. It's about wealth and power. It's about the rhythm of life—taking and giving. Above all, it's about the human spirit.

Here is a view of life as well as a way of life. The heart of the book is in the parables, with accompanying ponderings, grouped into "chapters." Some of the fables are hoary with age having gone through numerous incarnations over the millennia. A number of them were woven together from insights gleaned in my travels, discourses, and experiences. I believe this book will be easy to navigate for the dedicated seeker as well as for the curious inquirer.

The reader may choose different paths through the book. But I hope you will pause and reflect on the meaning from time to time. This is especially important in the beginning pages where the germinal ideas are presented. Some seekers will also discern scientific principles from environmental biology, public health, astrophysics, and related disciplines entwined with spiritual precepts. These precepts and practices have helped me redefine my self and my universe and I hope they will do as much for the reader.

A spiritual pilgrimage—travel to your center—usually proceeds in stages. At first, the destination may not be known but the direction is compelling. Different paths up the mountain all converge at the summit.

Ultimately, there is nowhere you have to go, nothing you have to attain. We already are what we most long to be. It is a matter of being, not a matter of becoming.

I invite you to join me in this epic journey toward Self discovery.


Rao Kolluru

# The Connection

It was a time when a rare alignment of celestial phenomena heralded the beginning of a new era.

It was a time when a majestic river meandered by a palace in Rampur of Distantland. In it lived Rama with his mother. He was born into Kshatriya lineage, rulers of those precincts. His father died when Rama was still a child.

As he was growing up, the prince dwelt many an hour on the banks of the river and in her depths. He would gaze at the river—ever changing, ever the same—at dawn and dusk, in sunshine and moonlight. She became his friend and mentor, his teacher and retreat. He often pondered whence the river came, whither she was going, what lay in her heart and soul. He wondered whether she had a beginning and an ending, birth and death. He wanted to know what the river's purpose was, whether she had any purpose at all.

By the time Rama was seventeen, he had memorized all the sacred scriptures by heart, performed all the rituals, mastered the skills of archery and swordsmanship, and studied the art of administration, as was customary of a Kshatriya prince. He grew up to be a handsome prince of lofty shoulders and keen intellect. His regal bearing and noble demeanor brought profound joy to the heart of his mother, and stirred deep passions in the bosoms of young maidens.

★

It so happened that one day, in the midst of storm and lightning, he was drawn by the sight of a personage sitting on the river bank, meditating. Rama joined him silently. Thereafter, they often meditated and performed ablutions together. Rama learned later that his friend, named Krishna, had taught medicine and metaphysics at a university. And that he had been at a monastic *Ashram* for many years in the mountains of Himarest. Rama didn't know where Krishna came from or how old he was. He seemed without place, without age. No matter. Rama rejoiced in the depths of Krishna's wisdom and the constancy of his bearing.

The two of them reflected often on the nature of man and God, on Self and ego, on joy and sorrow. On why Rama was born into privilege yet denied the love and assurance of his father. Whether the law of Karma was immutable. Much was revealed in these reflections, which assuaged Rama's intellectual curiosity. But the prince hankered after the real thing, not its shadow.

The seeds of discontent had begun to germinate. Rama yearned for peace; he wanted to know what it was like to be empty of pleasures and passions, joy and sorrow, desires and attachments. He longed to be free of the ego, to let the ego go.

✯

One day, they were sitting under a Cedar tree in the grove by the river. Krishna told Rama about a pilgrimage soon to take place. A score of seekers from a neighboring village would be embarking on a pilgrimage to the holy river Ganges. The prince needed little persuasion to join the pilgrimage. He had never before ventured far from his palace. He sensed his search unfolding.

Rama went to his mother's room that night to seek permission for a quest that would take him afar. His mother entreated him not to go, reminding him that he would soon be called upon to assume his princely duties. He stood still, gazing into emptiness. She saw in his demeanor a foreboding that she was about to lose him, that he might not return. Her heart was overwhelmed with grief. She broke into tears and wept helplessly.

Finally, he lay prostrate at her feet. It was then she realized that her love could not bind him. He had already left. She blessed him and gave her consent to pursue his calling, expressing the hope that some day he would come home and share with her his discoveries.

The next morning, Rama and Krishna met, wearing simple clothes befitting pilgrims. They hurried to the train station in the next town and joined the other pilgrims. It was a motley milieu, as different as they could be. Some were young but seemed to be suffering from some ailment. Others were old and in good spirits. Some had physical anomalies. Many brought everything from water to bedding, others carried nothing with them. All shared excitement of what lay in store. All desired one thing or another. Some wanted to merely get away from it all. A young couple sought to be blessed with a baby. Several were after worldly riches. A few were in quest of Nirvana.

In the evening, they boarded the train that would eventually bring them to faraway Varanasi on the banks of the sacred river Ganges. They all settled down, each laying claim to as much space as seemed reasonable. An elderly man with raspy voice started singing, soon joined by others. A few intoned the mantra Om. A palmist was reading the left hand of the young married woman, and assured her she was going to bear a boy. Yet others were meditating or slumbering as the train, with a loud whistle and a tug, pulled out of the station.

On the way, the train stopped at Pleasureville, where the passengers had to take a connecting train later that night. Rama and Krishna stayed at the station. Taking advantage of the break, the other passengers wandered into the city streets and plunged at once into the myriad worldly allures of the glittering city. Five passengers subsequently rejoined Rama and Krishna at the train station and continued their journey.

The train reached the next junction at Business City in late morning, delayed by flooding and landslides along the way. The passengers had missed the connecting train to Varanasi. The next train was not until that night. Rama and Krishna thought this would be a good time to find some food; they had not eaten that day or the previous day. The rumblings of hunger were getting louder. They collected two bowls from a charity booth at the station and wandered into the streets to beg for food. Rama felt strangely adventurous, not humbled in any way.

The others strolled into the city center and perceived extremely attractive business opportunities. They decided to stay on and work at expanding their worldly wealth. Of more than a score who had set out on the pilgrimage, only Krishna and Rama returned to the station and continued on at this time.

★

The train arrived at Varanasi the next morning. They needed no help to find Ganges. There was only one way they could go. Rama and Krishna joined the mass of hundreds of thousands and moved with them. Soon they became separated in the pull and tug of the throngs. Rama's heart missed a beat at the separation. He suddenly felt naked in his search even as he was being pressed on all sides by a sea of souls. He quickly regained his composure with the conviction that they would meet again and would have much to share.

When Rama reached Ganges, millions of the faithful had already congregated on her banks waiting to wade into the cleansing waters. He waited patiently for an opening; at last he found one, slipped into the water, and immersed himself. He felt a sudden release and a deep emptiness. He felt pristine.

When he opened his eyes, Rama was face to face with a yogi, who looked like an apparition. It seemed to be someone he had known forever, just as wings seem to know their wind. They both climbed the steps out of the water as if by a silent command from above.

The yogi picked up his staff and with Rama by his side, started threading his way through the throng of pilgrims. Without a word having been spoken they walked up the river the whole day, now and then withdrawing into the shade of a Banyan tree. They came upon the foothills, whence the sacred Ganges, River of a Thousand Tales, was born.

The Yogi and Rama sat down to rest under an ancient Bodhi tree. As the sun glided down the horizon leaving a faint glow, they got up and walked toward a hut nestled in a mango grove. They paused for a moment by a lotus pond. Then they collected some bananas and herbs and, sitting side by side in the twilight, consumed the food.

The Yogi and Rama slowly entered the hut and seated themselves on the straw mats that covered the floor. The Yogi did not speak but his face radiated wisdom and understanding, light and serenity. He produced a bracelet from somewhere and slipped it on to Rama's right hand.

In the stillness of night, embraced by the cool breeze from the river, they sat together and communed in silent reflections...

# Beginner's Mind: Getting in Touch with Our Origins

*Oh Lord…lead me*
*from the unreal to the real*
*from darkness to light*
*from death to immortality…*
    —*Brihadaranyaka Upanishad*

# Emptying the Mind

A RESPECTED PROFESSOR of science set out to unveil the mysteries of the Spirit. He journeyed to the foothills of Himarest, to a monastery by the sacred river Ganges. A senior monk there welcomed the professor, who seemed anxious to plunge into a discourse forthwith. Instead, the monk assigned him some manual tasks to perform in the monastery garden. And said that this day, "Day Zero" as he called it, would be devoted to emptying the mind. The monk advised the professor to observe total quiescence for the rest of the day. With these words, he withdrew to his quarters.

Next morning, the monk greeted the professor and invited him to a cup of tea before starting the discussions. He picked up the cup and the saucer, the cup resting upside down on the saucer, and started pouring tea from the tea pot. The tea flowed over and around the cup and spilled over the saucer.

Looking at the bewildered professor the monk said with a quizzical smile: "It is the emptiness of the cup that makes it useful. Just as a full cup or a closed cup does not accept any more tea, one cannot learn with a full mind, or with a preconceived mind. A beginner has infinite possibilities, an expert only a few."

∞

It is the empty valley that receives. It is the silent mind that listens.

The "empty" mind is the beginner's mind. It is pure, spontaneous, and boundless—the womb of infinite possibilities. This pristine mind is our natural heritage.

When the mind is filled with preconceptions, it becomes a divided mind, limited by its thoughts. Family, school, society—all foster knowledge that is bound by convention, custom, and prejudice. Attachment to such knowledge creates boundaries, "two minds" that limit the mind's potential.

The empty mind is not a blank mind. On the contrary, it is pure consciousness, in a state of infinite potentiality. Somewhat like the embryonic stem cells at conception, which have the potential to become any organ in the body—from brains to bones.

To catch a glimpse of the nature of the original mind, let us journey back in time to the cosmic womb that spawned the skies and the stars. To the moment when all this wondrous pageantry sprang forth from a single source, from virtual emptiness.

Let your mind's eye travel back further and further toward emptiness, to Time Zero. Get back in touch with the origins, the Source. Deep within us is a memory of that Source, like the lingering cosmic waves from the birth of the universe.

What is this Source? Reflect on it for a few silent moments...before pouring your tea.

# Of Mind, Matter, and Self: Who am I ?

> *The Self is everywhere*
> *Without a body, without a shape*
> *Whole, pure, wise, all knowing*
> *far shining, all transcending...*
> —*Esha (Esa) Upanishad*

# The Hidden Self

ONCE UPON A TIME, a team of angels decided to play a game of hide-and-seek with some new arrivals. But they couldn't decide on where to hide the Self. One angel suggested that they hide the Self way up in heaven where no man would ever find it.

On second thought, they decided that someone would eventually find it even there. Another angel suggested that they hide it in Limbo between heaven and earth, but again they discarded the idea because so many have come to live in Limbo.

Finally, the wisest of the angels suggested that they tuck the Self inside man. It would never occur to men to look inside; they would never find it there. After all, they were bestowed senses that only look out, not look in. Thus all the angels agreed to hide the Self inside man.

∞

A regal wave danced merrily on the sea, then looked down momentarily and realized it was one with the sea.

All human beings are aware of their bodies and minds—the seen and the unseen. Many have occasional glimpses of something else, something different, something beyond.

The physical body is the world of matter, perceived by the senses. The body is an ensemble of atoms and molecules, of energy and information. It is governed by the primal instincts of preservation and propagation. Ingenious as its architecture is, the biological body is bound, is finite.

At a subtler level is the mind, where we live in our every thought and emotion. It is not only a reservoir of memories, but also the theater of ideas and ideals that know no bounds. The mind is the medium of interplay between the physical and the metaphysical, the finite and the infinite. It is the key we use to unlock the inner universe.

What is at the center of the body and mind? Dwelling in the cave of everyone's heart is the subtlest of the subtle, the *self*. It is in the body, but not of it; waters cannot wet it, winds do not wither it. It has no beginning and no ending. This individual self in us is a projection of the universal *Self*. The Self that is immortal, immutable, infinite. The Self that is Godhead, the divine Spirit, the Source.

All of us are endowed with an individual body and a universal body, and all share the same *Source*. The individual selves are somewhat like waves in the vast ocean of the universal Self. Waves are unique in size, shape, and play but they all emanate from and merge with the same ocean.

Because we are so dedicated to looking out with our senses, we have lost access to our *Inner Being*. Nonetheless, the discovery of the self is open to all—devotees and skeptics alike.

Now and again a daring soul, longing for immortality, looks inward and finds him self.

# Not Your True Self

THE MAYOR OF GREAT CITY sought out a Monk well known for his connections with the cosmic Self, and requested an introduction. The Monk asked him who he was so he could introduce him to the Self. The mayor gave his name but the Monk pointed out that his name had been given to him by his parents and he wasn't born with it.

Then the mayor said he had been the mayor of Great City for ten years. The Monk asked who he was before becoming the mayor. He said he was a doctor by training. The Monk again pointed out that since his occupation or position had changed, that wasn't who he truly was. Truth never changes.

The perplexed mayor started to reflect on who he was not, in order to find out who he really was. Thus came about his introduction to his true self.

∞

The quest towards one's self is not a matter of attaining anything new. One need not go out and climb mountains in its pursuit. It is a matter of dis-covering, removing the covers.

Why don't we perceive the self within us? It is because of *Ahamkara*. Aham—the self, the real "I"—becomes attached to kara, the creation. The self—pure, whole, perfect—dwells in a transient physical habitat and comes to identify with that habitat, the body: I am man, woman, rich, poor, doctor, teacher, student, scientist, engineer, angry, happy, and so on. Such acquired habits of the mind are superimposed on the self.

We all play many parts on many stages. We identify with particular parts and often confuse the player for the part. Instead of enjoying the play for what it is, we become bounded by the part. Each part then adds another layer to the barrier that separates us from ourselves.

Although the individual self, *Atman*, is part of the universal Self, *Paramatman*, the self that dwells in a physical body takes on some of its trappings and is pulled away from the universal Self. In this way, the perception of our true identity, our ultimate Source, becomes clouded.

It is like gold which can be melted, drawn, and hammered into myriad forms—necklaces, bangles, rings, and a thousand other ornaments. Through it all, gold will remain gold. The nature of gold itself will not change.

The true nature of man, endowed with the Self, does not change. It is our awareness of who we are that changes. Eventually, the "I" feels the urge to break through the superficial layers and become free. Just like a child who plays with his toys and identifies with them; the child is temporarily distracted but eventually gets bored with the toys. Deep inside, the embodied self retains the yearning to return home, to unite with the Source and become Whole again—like rivers merging into the ocean, losing separate identities yet retaining their substance.

If you wish, you can visit the *Indweller* today without the masks and reintroduce yourself.

# The Seer Who Forgot to Look In

IN THE REMOTE VILLAGE OF SPIRITVILLE, there was a Seer who led a pious existence. One night, while he was reading his favorite scripture by candlelight, a vigorous rain storm blew out the flame. Realizing he had used up his last match, he picked up a kerosene lamp from a corner of the room, struggled over to his neighbor's house in the storm, and knocked on the door.

When the neighbor opened the door, the Seer apologized for disturbing him at that late hour, and requested to borrow matches to light his candle. Whereupon the neighbor exclaimed: "What a strange Seer you are. You have a lighted lamp in your own hands and you are searching all over for a match to light your candle!"

∞

Why not light the inner candle to illuminate the outer senses?

When you enter a dark room and turn on the light, the things that were already there are revealed. When one's heart and mind become still, the inner light that is turned on reveals the self that is always present.

We are like two "beings," the ego and the self. We can look out for the ego and we can look in for the self. Actually, it is not a matter of looking out or looking in, but looking rightly.

The ego—*Ahamkara*—divides the universe into two: "Me" and "not-me." The ego is not innate but an acquired "self." It offers a sense of order and security within narrow bounds. A rational ego identifies closely with the body and seeks to preserve a separate cocoon because therein lies its existence. Indeed, boundaries are necessary to preserve nature's diversity. That is what makes a rose a rose, an orchid an orchid.

Some people think of the ego as the outer self, lower self, or small self. The ego is neither good nor bad. We need simply to recognize its persona for what it is and acknowledge its limits. When the ego goes out of balance, one lives in the shadow of images, constantly seeking others' approval and validation, and solace in fleeting objects. What follows is preoccupation with images, acquisitions, and control. That sort of orientation depletes energy because it is based on fear and insecurity.

If you are connected with your inner self, the divine spirit, the desire for external control becomes trivial. The world of divisions and fears and scarcity gives way to one of unity, strength, and abundance. As the veils of ego are lifted, the confining thoughts dissolve to reveal a universe of peace and prosperity. As in sculpture, when the superfluous matter is chipped away, the inner beauty stands revealed.

Where is your center: Out there, or in here?

# Know Thy Self

ONCE UPON A TIME, in a forest adjoining a village, a lioness died shortly after giving birth to a cub. The cub was raised by sheep and became part of the flock. It started behaving like a sheep because of its company.

One day, while they were grazing, a lion came roaring out of the woods and jumped on the sheep causing them to run away. The lion amidst the sheep also started running away. This baffled the hunting lion that caught up with it and asked why it was running away. The sheepish lion mustered its courage and said it was afraid of being killed.

The invading lion understood what had happened and asked the other to follow him to a water hole. There, looking at its reflection alongside the other lion, the sheepish lion realized his original identity. He joined the other lion in a great roar as if to assert his true origins.

So too can man regain awareness of his true self by discarding false identities.

∞

Who are you, really?

There is some ambivalence to our identity. That is because we have some obvious things that are ever changing and a not so obvious something that is never changing.

Am I my body? If I am my body, then I am changing every second. Everything in the body, all the cells, are being constantly replaced, so that one becomes entirely "new" every seven years or so. Am I the body I was seven years ago, a moment ago, or what the body will become tomorrow?

The mind is constantly changing as well. The senses tell us that at different times we might be peaceful, angry, happy, greedy, generous, joyous, jealous, fat, slim, young, old, rich, poor, and so on. And we draw our identity from a collection of things: name, job, address, family, bank account, and the like. We live under assumed identities, wearing different masks for different occasions.

On the other hand, if I am not my body or mind, then to whom do they belong? Who is the one observing the body and mind? You cannot be what you possess and what you observe. The eyes cannot see themselves, nor can the brain feel its own pain or pleasure. Who, then, is this other being?

This other being is the Self—without qualifications, inscrutable, indefinable. The human mind cannot comprehend what is not created, the unborn that is not bounded by time and space. Any sort of definition would only be limiting. The ancient sages pondered this dilemma and proposed a succinct response: "not this, not that." We call this other "I" the Self or the Spirit.

You may have had a glimpse of this "I" on some occasions. Perhaps on your birthday—birthdays are special occasions for reflection—you looked deep into your eyes in a mirror, and sensed something that was always there. The *Indweller*—your self—hasn't changed. Always the same, ageless, despite the ever-changing facade.

Thus there are two aspects to our existence: constant change and changeless constancy. The realization that this "I," this self, is different from our outward expressions allows us to discriminate between the variable I and the invariable self. You are not simply the "old state," the "angry state," the "happy state," the "body you wear."

So, if I am not my body, if I am not my mind, if I am not my expressions, then who am I?

The body is like a chariot, the senses the horses, the mind the reins, the intellect the charioteer. The chariot will carry the seeker, if she perseveres, to the destination. This is the epic journey from the *creation* back to the *Creator*.

The self needs the body to enact the drama of life.

You are the eternal self on a worldly journey through your body and mind.

*That thou art.*

# The Three Universal Qualities: Elevating the Center

O God, by your Spirit tell us
what we need to hear,
and show us what we ought to do...
—*The Bible*

# Different Folks...

THERE WAS ONCE A GURU with two budding disciples named Rash and Timid. One day, Rash came to the Guru covered with bruises. He explained that a villain in the village was calling the Guru names, so he had beaten him up. The Guru expressed concern and said that Rash should have shown more restraint and let it pass.

Another day, Timid came to the Guru and complained of his encounter with a rogue in the village who maligned the Guru. He added that he didn't respond to the provocations. The Guru asked Timid why he didn't teach the rogue a lesson.

The two disciples were confused by the Guru's contradictory advice and concluded that he was not that wise after all. They decided to quit and packed their bags. But Mrs. Guru asked them to stay for a few minutes and have a cup of tea before they left. Then she explained the apparent inconsistency in the Guru's advice.

Your two natures are quite different. Rash, full of *Rajas* energy and passion, needed to cultivate *Sattva* tolerance and magnanimity. Timid, on the other hand, being centered in *Tamas* inertia, is meek and hesitant. He needed to engage in decisive action to strengthen his Rajas qualities and attain the right balance.

∞

In all creation, there are three fundamental qualities or *gunas*: *Sattva*, *Rajas*, and *Tamas*. This trinity is *Light*, *Activity*, and *Inertia*. Or information, energy, and mass. Sattva predominates in sunlight, Rajas in thundering storm, Tamas in a block of granite.

Sattva is enlightenment, magnanimity, and harmony. Rajas is expressed in actions, results, and attachment to fruits of actions. Tamas is darkness, lethargy, and absorption of energy. It is the Rajas energy that propels the world. Sattva balances the opposing traits of Rajas and Tamas. Rajas is action, Tamas is inaction, Sattva is union.

The influence of Rajas is manifest in creation, Sattva in preservation, Tamas in dissolution. A Sattvic person is tranquil and balanced with unitive spirit; he is guided by a sense of duty and untouched by triumph and failure. A Rajas person is energetic, motivated by wealth and power; driven by desires, he is quick to rejoice in success and despair in failure. A Tamas person dwells in darkness and sensual gratification; his heart is not in his deeds.

Where are you centered most of the time? It is not as if one is always better than the other. Sattva stillness, Rajas movement, and Tamas inertia are all necessary for creation. If there is no Tamas, there will be no rest. It's like the three basic colors—red, green, and blue—that merge to yield a rainbow of colors.

Whatever one's dominant tendency may be, it is possible to achieve a better balance by observing the play of the qualities. If one is imbued in Tamas inertia, he can add a little Rajas energy, consciously engaging in actions for personal and social benefit. One centered in Rajas may reflect and meditate to loosen the strings of attachment. Since most people tend to be centered in Tamas or Rajas, there is need to cultivate Sattva—through service, mindfulness, meditation, love, good company, humor, and the like.

A Sattvic person shares the light and helps others climb the mountaintop. Sattva-Rajas center brings forth enlightened action.

# Right Thoughts
# and Actions

DURING THE MONSOON SEASON, a yogi and his disciple were walking along a dirt path by a swollen river. They came upon a young girl in a colorful sari trying to cross a mud puddle. The yogi picked her up and carried her over the puddle, while the disciple watched the gesture in embarrassment.

After they reached the ashram, the embarrassed disciple asked why the yogi touched the pretty girl, after all, they had renounced all worldly pleasures. "I did what was needed at that moment. Why are you still carrying her?" said the yogi.

∞

Thoughts and speech are actions too. All actions are performed mentally and physically. The hand is an extension of the mind.

Actions are of three kinds: good, bad, and neutral or detached. Both good and bad actions are performed with expectations of results. Good and bad are preferences that depend on time and place. On the other hand, detached actions are spontaneous and universal, without regard to consequences. They leave no trace and incur no Karma.

Action of one kind or another is everywhere in creation, even in Sattva state. When a Sattvic person shares Sattva by his presence, that is action. A sage does without doing. Doesn't one feel magnanimous and buoyant in the presence of Sattva?

Most people think of action as just something physical performed by the body. But thoughts, even unspoken thoughts, produce vibrations similar to sounds. Such vibrations are creative, seeds or parents of actions, that sprout offspring in the garden of the mind. A tiny seed encapsulates all the potential of a huge tree. One who plants good thoughts harvests good actions. We create our own world, heaven and hell, by our own thoughts.

What is behind action? Most actions are driven by desires: desire for security, desire for sensual pleasures, desire for wealth and power, desire for enlightenment, desire for change.

But spontaneous actions are performed by pure consciousness before one's expectations get in the way. Such actions bypass the repertoire of deeply rooted beliefs and automatic responses. Spontaneous actions are rooted in the heart, whereas automatic responses stem from habits. Children are spontaneous and find it easy just to be.

Non-action is also a form of action. It is as important not to act when you should not, as to act when you need to. Inaction should be by choice. Sooner or later, everyone experiences the consequences of inaction, which can be even more far-reaching, becoming abundantly clear in retrospect.

You are at peace only when your thoughts, words and deeds are one. The constellation of thoughts, words, and deeds translates into habits, behavior, and character much like a path made in a garden by footprints. You are all of what you see, what you hear, what you think, what you speak, what you do.

See what is beautiful. Hear what is auspicious. Think what is right. Cultivate good company, Satsang. These lead to good thoughts, to increased Sattva, to good deeds. Just as the scent of the rose bush wafts and permeates the air far away, so the scent of a good deed will reach far and wide.

# Pretense, a Prelude to Change

THE PIOUS KING OF SAGEDOM wanted his daughter to marry a saint. He sent scouts on a mission to find a worthy candidate. The scouts headed to the banks of Ganga where sages would sit in meditation. Meanwhile, a veteran thief got wind of the king's intentions and disguised himself as a sage and sat along the river with the other sages.

When the scouts approached the sages and elicited their interest in the king's daughter, they were ignored. When they approached the thief in disguise, he said he would consider it.

The scouts returned to the king and reported that they found a sage who might marry the princess. So the king and the princess set out with the scouts to find the saint. When they found him, the king offered the princess's hand in marriage.

The thief pondered what had happened. If a fake saint was bestowed this kind of honor, what could a real saint receive?

In time, the thief came to be known as Ramadas, the servant of Rama, an Avatar of the God Vishnu.

∞

The power to transform is latent in us all.

When the time is ripe, there is instant transformation. The change can also be gradual as it comes about through thought, speech, and action. You can alter your thinking by deliberately speaking or acting in a certain way, just as the clothes you wear affect the way you behave. Action is powerful medicine. The right action purifies the mind.

Befriend the mind. What a strange being it is! When turned outward, the wandering winds of the senses cast the mind adrift. The mind breeds thoughts and images day and night. It longs for summer in winter and for spring in summer. It isn't happy until it has everything, and unhappy when it has everything. But when the senses are drawn in, when the mind turns inward, the same mind becomes still and melts into your self.

Good company causes good tendencies that result in good actions. The expression of good thoughts and deeds is welcome, but then you become unwittingly what you think and what you experience. These veneers, beautiful though they may be, are impurities that pull you off your center. They must be cast off through daily meditation, like an actor who must occasionally go backstage to remember who he really is.

Man's true nature, anchored in the Self, cannot be changed. On the other hand, we can change the daily balance of Sattva stillness, Rajas movement, and Tamas inertia and become centered in Sattva. Since Sattva is part of creation and can be depleted, it should be replenished everyday through meditation, prayer, good company, and rightful action.

Old habits pull us back again and again, but we can emerge from them and change.

# The Material
# and the Spiritual:
# One or Both?

*Dost thou think, because thou art virtuous,*
*there shall be no more cake and ale?*
—*Shakespeare*, Twelfth Night

# When Is Enough?

IN THE ANCIENT KINGDOM of Mayaland, the Minister at the King's Court was walking home through woods one evening. While he was passing under the Celestial Tree, a voice asked him if he wanted seven pots of gold. Skeptical, but curious, he said yes. The fairy voice said his wish was granted and that he would find the gold when he went home.

When he entered his home, there were indeed the seven pots of gold coins, but the seventh was only three-quarters full. Disappointed at the shortfall, he started to cut down expenses, starved himself and his family, and purchased gold coins to fill the seventh pot. The pot devoured the coins and the void remained as ever. The Minister then approached the King and beseeched him to raise his remuneration. The King had always been pleased with the Minister's faithful services and, sensing that he was in some sort of dire strait, doubled his remuneration.

The Minister dutifully deposited his new riches into the pot, still to no avail. His plight grew desperate day by day and noticing this, the King asked him if he had by chance got the seven pots of gold. Taken aback by this observation, the Minister asked the King how he knew of it. The King said that the Minister was showing all the symptoms of having fallen victim to the Gold Fairy. The King himself had nearly become a victim at one time but, by a flash of insight, asked the Gold Fairy if he could use the gold—or was he required only to hoard it? Whereupon the Gold Fairy disappeared without further ado.

Having been so enlightened, on his way home, the Minister asked the same question of the Gold Fairy under the Celestial Tree. When he returned home, the Minister found that all the gold had vanished. He suddenly felt a great burden lifted from his shoulders.

∞

To know when is enough, you need to know what is more than enough. Which weight is worse to bear, too much or too little?

Life is a constant search for a balance between "what is" and "what ought to be," between "doing" and "being," between having one thing and having it all.

Spirituality is not a retreat from the material province. There are a few famous yogis on the mountains above, but many more urban yogis living in the valleys below. Material poverty is welcome only if chosen deliberately out of free will. You have to be somebody before you can become nobody.

Gold and other things are not good or bad in and of themselves. It is your attachment that confers power on them. Detachment or disidentification from fleeting objects is the road to freedom.

In some villages, monkeys are caught by a simple trick. Bananas are put in a heavy metal pot with a narrow opening and placed by a tree. A monkey comes down the tree and grabs the banana in the pot but cannot get its hand out through the small opening. Clinging to the banana, not letting go, the monkey loses its freedom.

Material success symbolized by wealth, fame, and power involves social interaction and extends beyond the purely personal domain. What matters is whether the worldly wealth and power are acquired by the right means and used for the right purpose. This kind of success is of a higher order than purely personal pleasures because it is for the common good.

Nevertheless, material success is finite and insatiable. Trying to satisfy the thirst for riches by yet more money is like trying to quench a fire by pouring oil on it. Isn't the fear of thirst when one's well is full unquenchable?

One can be immersed in fame and fortune, yet be tormented by feelings of emptiness, by a feeling of being an "impostor." Some people assume there is no other way. Others search for their place and purpose in life.

Sooner or later the question arises: What next? What else? What do I really want?

# Go Further...

A MERCHANT who had amassed great wealth in Utopica returned to his homeland and built a palatial house in Nothingville. One day, he was looking out from his balcony and noticed a yogi sitting on top of a hill nearby. He felt the urge to make the yogi's acquaintance and sent one of his servants to invite him to dinner.

The servant got back and told the merchant that the yogi would not come. The merchant, though disappointed, thought that it was the yogi's loss, having missed out on a sumptuous meal.

Several days went by and the merchant again felt the urge to meet with the yogi. He made his way up the hill and greeted the yogi with some resentment for making him climb all the way. The yogi, wearing nothing but a loincloth, asked what the merchant wanted.

The merchant said his ambition was to bring prosperity to Nothingville. "I will plant new seeds on all the land around here and grow plenty of food." "Then what?" asked the yogi. "Then I will build a factory and provide jobs for the people." "What happens then?" repeated the yogi. "I will build roads and theaters and temples." "What then?" the yogi persisted. "Well, then nothing" said the merchant in exasperation.

"I am already nothing and desire nothing," said the yogi.

∞

In order to reach the pinnacle, one must shed excess baggage and ultimately all baggage.

Most people want peace and happiness. And they think they will be happy when they have this or become that, then the next, the next, and so on. Where is the time to be happy?

People look to things and persons to find pleasure and happiness. External objects and relationships can give moments of pleasure, and there is nothing wrong with it. Pleasure objects are gripping until you experience them. Once you experience them, they are no longer special. How lasting, for example, is the taste of strawberry ice cream?

Pleasure and pain, like day and night, shadow each other. Pleasure of having something and pain of losing it; pleasure of possessing and pain of seeing someone possess even more. If possessions are one's security blanket, if one is possessed by his possessions, the thought of their loss brings misery.

Beyond food and shelter, people seek fame and fortune and power. The wealth and power anchored in the outer world is fine as far as it goes, but one will always find somebody who has more money or more power. People are always comparing—with neighbors, with the past, with friends and relatives.

Your body, your mind, the extent of your possessions are all changing moment to moment.

The problem is that we think we are only the body, or the mind, or the extent of our possessions. When the body is sick, I am sick; when the body is handsome, I am handsome; when the body is old, I am old; when I have few possessions, I am poor; and so on. Consequently, the "I" is subjected to, and limited by, the states of the body and the mind.

On the other hand, if you turn inward and reconnect with your self, you will find that there are no limits, no competition. No one— absolutely no one—has more than your self; it is pure, perfect, and complete. Your happiness will not depend on outside circumstances. And the self is always present—no one can take it away from you.

# On Spiritual Quest

A RELIGIOUS SEEKER went on a pilgrimage to holy places near and far. Upon returning to his village, he went to the temple one evening. The Brahmin priest asked him about his sojourn. The seeker said he had visited numerous temples and had participated in innumerable spiritual discourses. "But God still eludes me," he sighed in exasperation.

The Brahmin was preparing for the evening worship and asked him to fetch jasmine flowers from a shop at the other end of Main Street. He filled a flat plate with ceremonial water and asked the seeker to take it with him and not to spill even a drop of water. The seeker was puzzled at the injunction but proceeded to do what the Brahmin asked him.

When the seeker returned with the flowers, the Brahmin asked him to go back and bring some chrysanthemums and take the plate of water with him again. Much annoyed at having to make the trip again, he nevertheless yielded, suspecting something was afoot.

When he returned with the chrysanthemums, the Brahmin asked him whether the fun fair on the Main Street was open. He said he didn't notice. "How is the dancing by the temple courtesans in the open theater at the Civic Center?" Again the seeker said he didn't see anything because he had to concentrate on his plate of water with unwavering mind; he couldn't let himself be distracted by the side shows.

"You have to focus on God the same way you focused on the water in the plate," said the Brahmin with an understanding smile. "It may be your longing for God is not intense enough. God needs to know whether you are simply trying to attract attention like a toddler temporarily bored playing with his toys. He'll wait until you passionately want and need him. Until he is not just one of the choices, but the only choice."

∞

The journey to your self usually proceeds in stages: searching for the footprints of the "lost" self, discerning the path, perceiving the self, returning home. Different seekers start at different stages. At first, the destination may not be known but the direction is compelling.

The pilgrimage often begins with a personal crisis, a call from within to travel a different path. As many aspirants, so many paths to spirituality: Dharma, Karmic action, meditation, yoga, devotion, knowledge, humor, service, right teacher, good associations, and the like. You travel the path that beckons, best suited to the inclinations of your heart and mind. The contemplative may prefer the path of knowledge, the energetic the path of active service. Different paths up the mountain all converge at the summit.

A traveler, with miles to go at night, feared traveling with a lamp that lighted only a few feet, then realized that was all he needed. Similarly, a sincere seeker will discern the light within will illuminate the path ahead as she takes each step. Can you separate the peacock from its dance?

Even though man created God in his own image, most people view God as impersonal, if not imperious. Indeed, it would put a great strain on most mortals to have an omnipotent and omniscient God in constant company. A personal god can make the spirit come alive to build an intimate relationship. It is easier to relate to a Buddha, Christ, or Krishna than to a nameless and formless God. They are God's *Avatars*, symbolizing God but reduced to human form, incarnating human foibles.

You may have some favorite personal deities. They can be spiritual icons from scriptures, guardian angels, prophets and other sentient beings, your ancestors, or your Guru. Each deity personifies certain qualities like love, wisdom, courage, and material riches. You may invoke the deities for guidance and to bring out their qualities within you.

Faith in an absolute God and a family of deities is in harmony with humanity's dual existence: *being* and *becoming*. The need for constancy, something you can always count on, ultimate refuge. And the need for change—to venture, to dare, to hope. The relationship with your deities is devotional as well as playful. It is also helpful to keep close a talisman from a spiritual Guru as a visible reminder of the deity's presence by you.

Along the way, you need Good Company—*Satsang*—to partake of Sattva and illuminate the path in front. Just as a sapling requires careful tending to take root and grow into a tree, a beginner needs structure and support—symbols, rituals, shared interests, fellow celebrants of the spirit. Rituals satisfy the heart's longing for rhythm, while the mind thrives on adventure. Occasional retreats nurture both. One might visit temples of beauty and tranquillity, especially on holidays—holy days. Good company—be it an exotic flower, exquisite painting, captivating music, beautiful person, or a succinct mathematical equation—draws us closer to the Source.

The journey—from the ephemeral to the enduring to the eternal—is often mired in a web of desires. Desires cause anxiety and confusion. Too many material desires slow spiritual progress like detours on a highway. Mindfulness and meditation take time away from desires and worries—giving way to simple living. As one becomes freer and freer of sense objects, a new vision of higher truth will begin to unfold.

Both faith and doubt are essential to spiritual unfolding. The saying that "I will believe it when I see it" is a bit backwards. Instead, we see it when we believe it. We see things not as they are but as we are. Faith strengthens the will. Doubts leave open the possibility of change. When doubts appear along the way, often triggered by the ego's insecurity, welcome them to delve deeper into truth.

Despite all the worldly distractions, it is possible to create an island of peace within and live from a calm center. The mind's static will gradually settle down and the island will expand little by little into a peaceful world. The deep ocean is unruffled by surface turbulence.

Meditation everyday can help you drop the trappings of daily living and reawaken the memory of the Spirit. In meditative stillness, you give up everything—your feelings, your thoughts, your time—and offer all to the Source. Meditation practices vary widely. One can meditate twice a day—twenty minutes or so in the morning and in the evening, or more often for a few minutes each time, mingling meditation with daily life. You may also observe a day of silence, bypassing the urge to speak. True spirituality is a mental attitude that can be practiced any time, all the time.

Occasional glimpses of the infinite and the moments of peace and bliss will increase in frequency, duration, and intensity as you come closer to your self.

Ultimately, there is nowhere you need to go, nothing to attain. We already are what we most longed to be. Our quest, our purpose in life, is to regain our original identity, to return home. It is a matter of being, not a matter of becoming.

# Of Dharma, Duties and Actions: Doing the Right Thing

*The Lord said*

*Do your duty and you shall prosper*

*Action rightly performed brings freedom…*

*Fruits rightly renounced bring*

*enlightenment…*

*Bhagavad Gita*

# Life-cycle Stages and Duties

THERE ONCE WAS A FARMER who worked diligently to make a living. He would deposit his modest income into three pots on a shelf in the kitchen, marked Grandparents, Family, and Daughter. One evening, as the Farmer was depositing the money separately into the three pots, his young daughter asked why he was doing that.

The Farmer explained that the money in the Grandparents Pot is to pay off a debt to them, to support them in their old age. The money in the Family Pot is to pay for the family's current needs of food and shelter. The Daughter Pot of savings is to invest in her education to prepare for her future career. "You, in turn, will soon be launching your own three pots when you grow up," he said.

∞

Traditionally, a person's life cycle duties encompassed four stages spanning a century—somewhat like the four seasons of nature. These stages, or *Ashramas*, are called *Student, Householder, Hermit,* and *Renouncer.*

In the first stage, the first 25 years or so, family and society invest in the "student" furnishing physical, mental, and spiritual nourishment. In this stage, the student's primary focus is education, training, and character development—to be all he can be, to prepare for family and work career, the staple of human life.

In the householder stage, from about 25 to 50 years, the focus shifts to work, economic enterprise, fulfilling the genetic proclivities and raising a family. In this family and work stage, the person brings up children, cares for parents' needs, and shares the fruits of his work with society. This stage is particularly important to the well-being of society.

The advanced stages are a time for service and reflection. Work continues but there may be a career change and a reinventing of oneself. Man creates and recreates himself through his work. The emphasis shifts from work to service. The nuclear family becomes an extended family including grandchildren, one's own and those of others. From grandparents to grandchildren is a good channel of wisdom. By middle age, one's technical knowledge may become outdated. Not so with wisdom.

The autumn of life is the time to cultivate detachment from possessions and share more and more worldly wealth with the family, society, and the planet. One can of course become a renouncer, *Sannyasa,* at any age or stage. Usually, as one grows old he becomes young again like a child, drawing sustenance from the family and the society. The engagement of self intensifies. And it's a time to prepare for a dignified transition, reflecting on the encores.

# Of Brahman and Brahmin

A WORKER born into a low caste one day felt the urge to pray and went to the village temple. But he was turned away by the Brahmin priest since he belonged to the caste of untouchables. Disappointed and resentful, he approached a holy man who was sitting under a Banyan tree outside the temple, and sat at his feet.

The holy man discerned what had happened and spoke to the untouchable. And he said: After Brahma created the universe, he thought it to be a good idea to have a society of people to perform the different tasks. First he projected Brahmin priests but they did not prosper by themselves. So he created Kshatriya rulers; they too did not flourish. Then he projected Vaisya merchants, still to no avail. And then he projected Sudra workers. Thus the society had a good balance of natural qualities in educators, rulers, merchants and workers. But there was something missing still. Finally, he bestowed the society with Dharma, code of duties, to bind the disparate groups.

As the untouchable was walking away, the thought came to him that performing his duties to the best of his ability was the best prayer.

∞

Mankind has four kinds of natural inclinations or qualities. *Brahmins* are contemplative and spiritually inclined. *Kshatriyas* are endowed with warrior and executive qualities. *Vaisyas* are talented in matters of money, trade, and agriculture. *Sudras* have predilection for crafts and manual labor.

Initially, caste was not hereditary. People of similar aptitudes and inclinations tended to group together. The caste structure evolved in early societies to fulfill social needs as structure gave meaning and purpose. Brahmins, the knowers of Brahman or God, came to be predominantly priests, educators, and ministers; their duty was to perform religious ceremonies and teach Vedas. The duty of Kshatriyas was to protect the people from aggressors, administer justice, and maintain peace. Vaisyas worked to improve the wealth of the country. Sudras and other commoners engaged in production using bodily labor. The four groups functioned as one mind for the welfare of the society.

The caste system provided a dynamic balance as well. The "pen" of the scholars, the "sword" of the warriors, the money of the merchants, and the skills of the "laborers" offered a power balance. Modern societies have devised a slightly different set of balancing elements, usually legislative, executive, judicial, and financial. These work well when they flow with the natural human propensities and not against them.

Although the caste system served a useful purpose for thousands of years, over time, some castes acquired special privileges. Not surprisingly, they wanted to perpetuate these privileges regardless of their contribution to society. These vested interests led to a rigid hierarchy.

The new societies need a balance of hierarchical structures and self-organizing, fluid networks—a balance of tradition and innovation.

# The Ascetic
# and the Village Sweep

AN ASCETIC practiced meditation day and night in a forest and acquired great powers of concentration. However, one day while meditating, he was disturbed by the noise of a mongoose chasing a snake. He looked upon them with annoyance as if they had no business disturbing someone engaged in such high purpose. No sooner had the thought crossed his mind than both animals dropped dead. This greatly impressed the ascetic who had not seen such devastating power even in his own Guru.

Since he had not eaten for several days, the ascetic got up and walked to a nearby village and knocked on the door of a house. When a woman opened the door, he requested some food. The woman asked him to wait and went back in. A long time passed, and when the woman finally returned, he looked at her with anger for making him wait. She apologized for the delay because she had to give food to her family and help her daughter with homework. Looking at his angry face, she added: "I hope you won't direct your powers to harm anyone as you did in the forest."

Flabbergasted, but intrigued by her uncanny power to read his mind, the ascetic asked who her Guru was. She said, "When I approached my childhood Guru to study and serve under him, he advised me to return home and fulfill my family duties in this stage of my life." But the ascetic, coveting yet more powers, insisted on knowing who her Guru was. Then she told him.

It was well into dusk when the ascetic reached the next village. He was greeted by the Guru, a street cleaner, covered by dust, still at work. "Why have you come here carrying so many burdens?" asked he. "You became conceited when you thought you acquired extraordinary power. You became confused when you found a housewife with even greater powers. Now you are distressed with this encounter because I am a mere street cleaner."

∞

True power lies not in occult acts but in fulfilling Dharma—code of duties, purpose in life—that comes from creation by virtue of one's birth.

The three levels of Dharma are universal, social, and personal. Their fulfillment varies with the different stages of life, echoing life's rhythm of taking and giving—more taking in the early stages of life and more giving in the later stages to balance out.

Universal Dharma is the divine law that sustains cosmic order prevailing at every level of existence, even obligations to our habitat as guests on this planet. Social Dharma embraces the duties and responsibilities to family and society.

Personal Dharma and duties extend outward in spheres. First you are responsible for your thoughts, words, and actions—your mind and body. You are responsible for self-actualization, being all that you can be. Another duty is toward your family. You have an obligation in two directions: to that from which you have come, your forebears, and to which you have contributed, your progeny.

# Actors and Agents

ONCE UPON A TIME, a Rishi sat in a forest and prayed ceaselessly day and night without any food. God decided to send her some food and called one of his messengers. The messenger said there was a slight problem because the Rishi was on the other side of an immense river and he had no means to cross it at this time.

God said that all he needed to do was to make any true statement and the river would part. "For instance, that I am celibate." This baffled the messenger in as much as this particular god incarnate was reputed to have several playful companions. Nevertheless, when he reached the river, the messenger repeated the statement and the river parted, allowing him to cross.

After giving food to the Rishi, the messenger again faced the problem of having to cross the river. The Rishi advised him to say that she always fasted, even though she had just then consumed a sumptuous meal. The messenger repeated her statement and the river parted allowing him to cross back.

Soon he understood the apparent paradox: Enlightened actions performed in detachment, where the fruits of efforts are offered to God, do not bind the actor as water does not cling to the lotus leaf. The actor is not always the agent.

∞

Non-attachment to action does not mean non-action or indifference. And it doesn't mean one is above one's actions.

Actions are of two kinds—"offerings" and "takings." Actions performed without attachment to fruits are offerings. They emanate from Sattva and reinforce the Sattva spirit. Actions performed with attachment to results are takings, and reinforce Rajas passion.

Non-attachment to the fruits of your actions doesn't mean you are denied the fruits. Because man plants the seed to harvest its fruit, detachment from expectations of rewards, *holy indifference*, doesn't come easily and has to be cultivated.

Action is the central element of the trinity: Dharma, Action, Results. Dharma or duty comes from creation. Action is what you do to actuate the potential and fulfill your Dharma. Results and rewards are the domain of a higher order, not in your control.

Actions bear fruit through intention, attention, and manifestation. Specific goals are needed to set the course and pace. Remember, too, goals should be enabling, not limiting. Intention, the goal, is energized by attention, the action, into material expression. But there is a difference between actions and results. Efforts are made by the body's instruments. Results are the domain of a higher order, the transcendent Self.

One who broods over the outcome, weakens the income. Is the actor present or absent while acting? When the actor's attention is not in the present moment but on future rewards, then that energy is not available for the action at hand.

Recall the freedom and peace you experienced on occasions when you gave up all striving and let your free consciousness do the doing.

# Mindfulness and Meditation: Being Present in the Present

*Be still and know that I am God.*

—*The Bible*

# The Monk and His Moment

A MONK was walking through a forest one day and suddenly came upon a tiger poised to pounce on him. He ran over to a nearby cliff and slid over the side hanging by a tenuous vine. Looking down the ravine below, he noticed several crocodiles in a river looking up in anticipation.

Facing what seemed like certain death, the hapless monk, mindful of the moment, noticed luscious berries hanging nearby. He plucked and savored them to his heart's content.

∞

You are "mind full" when you fill the mind with what is here now, fully present in this moment. When you are not in this moment, you are part of the past or the future.

Being mindful is to connect with the senses, the mind-body connection. Since our senses work only in the present, when you connect with the senses, you come into the present—consciously experiencing everything as if for the first time, with a Beginner's Mind, like a child in awe of everything. That way you can witness the hidden drama in the most mundane and savor the "present."

What is unique about the present moment? All that you are, all that you have, is in this moment and nowhere else. It is always NOW, the *eternal moment*. When you open up your senses and give out full attention to whatever is at hand, the pure awareness frees the mind from the circling thoughts and the internal monologue, from the cacophony of the mind. Paradoxically, when you become one with the object of your attention, the sensory world doesn't exist, nothing else exists.

To be fully aware of what is present, it is necessary to suspend all judgment. It is "what is," leaving "what ought to be" to a higher order. You can really see and smell the roses only when you are not thinking about roses.

Some people wait all their lives for the future to arrive, rehearsing the past and the future, bypassing the present entirely. Children are naturally mindful, whereas most grownups cruise through the day on autopilot, in a sort of waking dream state, living in the shadows of the past or the future. Their bodies are present but their minds are absent.

Pure awareness heightens the value of whatever you do be it reading, listening, or playing. And things shouldn't have to be special for you to pay attention. They can be such everyday events as eating and bathing. Perhaps people would eat less if they were more mindful of what they were eating, and remembered what and when they had eaten.

Living in the moment doesn't mean living for the moment. It is not as if you should not reflect on the past to learn useful lessons or to reinforce an experience. Nor that you should not dream or plan for the future. People have always harbored the desire to rewrite their past. In a way, you can. The present is here to repair the past and prepare the future.

Don't be in front of the present, or behind. Free the mind for the present.

I'm Here Now.

# The Pause
# that Refreshed

ONCE UPON A TIME, a devotee sat under a Tamarind tree
and prayed relentlessly day and night in sun and rain. One
of God's aides wanted to see how deep was the devotee's
concentration. He summoned storms and floods that
deluged the whole place, but the devotee continued his
meditation. Then the aide turned into Apsara, the most
beautiful girl in the universe, and danced seductively in
front of the devotee. Still the devotee continued to be
mindful of God, oblivious of the enchantress.

The aide gave up and approached God for advice. At
God's behest, down he flew as His emissary and waited
patiently for the devotee to open his eyes. When he did,
the emissary offered his salutations and asked what it was
that the devotee wanted. He wanted to know when God
was going to appear. The emissary consulted with God and
came back with the message: "God will appear in as many
years as there are leaves on this Tamarind tree."

Upon hearing those words, the devotee jumped up and
started dancing and singing in great jubilation. Perplexed,
the emissary repeated his message and pointed out that
there are millions of leaves on the Tamarind tree. The

devotee continued with his dancing saying: "What does it matter as long as I have heard from God?"

Suddenly there was lightening and thunder and God himself appeared before the devotee. The emissary, feeling a little embarrassed, asked why God had not kept his word. "To a single-minded devotee with such faith" said God, "time stops."

∞

The pause is a restful interlude that comes to us from the Creator. It's like an actor going backstage during intermission to renew himself.

All activities have a beginning and an ending. When you pause between activities, the Rajas energy raised and depleted in the previous activity is restored, just like a well that becomes replenished if left unused for a time.

Even thoughts are a form of action. A person thinks thousands of thoughts every day. Despite the constant chatter of the mind, one can only think one thought at a time. When one thought is past and the future thought has not yet arisen, there is a gap, a virtual emptiness. This gap, however small, can be seized and stretched by inserting a deliberate pause—a deep breath, a moment of silence, the seventh day of rest.

The pristine *emptiness* of the natural mind, called *Rigpa,* is a liberating moment, a moment of infinite potentiality. Let this potentiality take root and grow through meditation. Indeed, meditation is an eternal pause.

Pause often. Act-pause. Think-pause. Pause-eat. Pause.

# Holy Man and the Courtesan

THERE WAS A HOLY MAN who lived across the street from a prostitute. He was much disturbed by her way of life. Even as he worshipped, every time a customer walked through her front gate, he would make a checkmark and kept a daily count as a visible reminder of her immoral life.

It so happened that they both died at the same time from a natural event and ended up at heaven's gate together. The gatekeeper signaled the prostitute to pass right through but stopped the holy man and pointed him in the other direction. The holy man protested and said that the gatekeeper must have his signals crossed.

"Not so" said the gatekeeper, "the prostitute was mindful of her occupation and performed her duty with devotion. Although you engaged in many hours of prayer, your mind was not centered in God. You indulged in scrutinizing her activities not for her benefit but for your own, to make youself feel superior. In contrast, every time the prostitute looked at you and your abode, she was filled with holy thoughts."

∞

Mindfulness, meditation, prayer—all preclude judgment.

Prayer and meditation do not make a person holy. Holy men do not entertain thoughts of "holier than thou."

The human penchant for judging and categorizing everything and everyone as good or bad, likable and not likable, and so on, robs us of the moment, and prevents us from seeing them as they are.

Likes and dislikes lead to divisions. Where there are divisions, there are conflicts. Where there are conflicts, how can there be peace and happiness?

When one meditates, he becomes one with the Self, and sees the Self in everyone. When we meditate, we meditate for all mankind—restoring the natural balance that is being lost in the quickening pace of life.

In shared silence, we all speak the same language.

When the mind is still, when it is lost in silence, where is it gone?

# The Natural Mind

ON THE EVE OF THE NEW MILLENNIUM, a young student who had a short temper got the urge to reform himself. He was referred by friends to a saint in a nearby hermitage.

The student approached the saint and requested his advice on how to cure his temper. The saint asked him to show his bad temper. "But I'm only angry when I feel fearful or jealous; it only happens sometimes, not right now," said the student.

"Aha," said the saint, "if anger is not with you all the time, it's not really you. It is an anomaly, a mere bubble of the mind. You are never without your inherent nature."

∞

Anger, fear, hatred, and other negative emotions are not natural states of mind. They'll pass, if you let them.

The natural mind is pristine, clear and transparent—pure consciousness. At the beginning it's like pure water. A colored mind colors everything it receives.

If there is turbid water in a bottle, the contaminant particles will settle down if left undisturbed. First the heavy particles, then the lighter particles, until the water above becomes fully clear. The mind is like the water that needs stillness to reveal its true nature.

The human mind becomes colored and turbid and divided by family, school, experience, expectancy. A mind so "loaded" makes day-to-day living easier. But to awaken the innate *Buddhi*, the faculty of pure reason and understanding, we have to practice emptying the mind regularly, becoming "ignorant" again and again.

What flows through the mind is affected not only by birth and experience but also by its present state. In Sattva light, we perceive and reflect the truth as is. Rajas agitated state produces some distortions and rationalizations. In Tamas darkness, ignorance is seen as truth.

The natural mind is like the sky—open, free, boundless. It deals freely and spontaneously with whatever is present without clinging—like a mirror not covered by dust will reflect everything before it without being affected by it.

Mind is the springboard but is not itself thoughts or experiences.

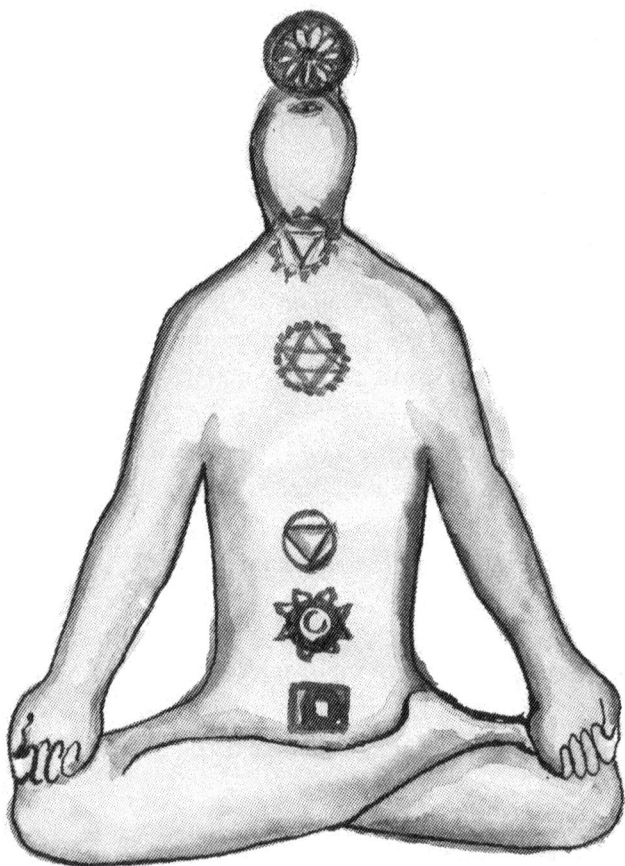

# Consciousness, Metaconsciousness, and the Universal Mind

*Om, Infinite is that, infinite is this. From the Infinite proceeds the infinite...*

— Brihadaranyaka Upanishad

# Who Is
# the Real Ganga?

A LONG, LONG TIME AGO, a beautiful baby was born to a Brahmin couple in Varani. Since she was born by the holy river Ganga, she was christened Ganga. She and Rahul—the son of a schoolteacher—grew up together. In time, they fell deeply in love and vowed to share the rest of their lives together. Their parents also wished that they would get married.

One day, a traveler going up the river in a boat saw Ganga bathing in the river. He fell in love with her at first sight. When he reached home, he told his parents what had happened, and that she was the only girl he would marry. His parents made inquiries and sent a mediator to Ganga's parents with the offer of a hundred gold coins as dowry. Ganga's parents could not resist the offer and agreed to the marriage.

Ganga and Rahul were heartbroken at this twist of fate. They decided to elope that night. They took a boat to a town down the river and settled there. There they had a son and led a joyous life.

Still, as years went by, they felt something missing. They missed the connection with their families. So they decided to visit their families and traveled to Varani. When they reached Ganga's childhood home, Rahul asked her to wait outside so he could go in first and seek forgiveness from her parents. When Rahul went in, he saw Ganga's father and started to apologize for running away from home.

The father was perplexed and in tears at Rahul's atonement. He took Rahul to the next room where Ganga was lying in bed. How could this be, Rahul wondered. The father said she had fallen ill the moment she heard the news that she was to be married to a stranger, and had been languishing in bed without consciousness all these years.

Who is the real Ganga: The unconscious body in bed, or the woman who ran away and returned with a son?

∞

What is a body without consciousness?

It is the light of consciousness that animates the body, that makes it sentient. You are consciousness. The whole universe is in your consciousness.

Like energy that has perpetual life but takes on various guises, consciousness is like a lake with different depths, each with its own life forms.

Your level of awareness depends on your state of consciousness. The first level is an awareness of your surroundings with your senses, which only work in the present. Thus, awareness is always in the present, while consciousness is not bounded by time. The next level is an awareness of being aware. To be conscious of being conscious is metaconsciousness. This is like the enigma of the eye observing itself seeing.

Most of the time, we experience three ordinary states of consciousness: the conscious awake state with awareness of external surroundings; the subconscious state where perceptions are turned inward as in dreams; and the deep unconscious state of deep sleep. There is consciousness all the time since we can recall our dreams and wake up from sleep.

In the awake state, you are aware of gross objects, of pleasure and pain, mainly through the sense organs. In the dream state, you experience subtle impressions illumined by the subconscious mind. In deep sleep, you penetrate the innermost self and rest in its depths—free of ego, free of all striving, free of the usual limits of time and space and form. In deep sleep, everyone becomes a yogi. Freed of all attachments, the consciousness decompresses to infinity. Pure consciousness, always the same.

In other words, consciousness is like space, always there. The space inside your room is bounded by walls and ceilings. If you open the window, you will uncover more space. Step outside your home and look up, still more space. When you open the "mind's eye," there is infinite inner space.

Meditation and a sense of humor are helpful in opening the gateless gate of higher consciousness. In this consciousness is unity: cause and effect, actions and results, sun and moon, man and nature, creator and creation—all converge to one. *Advaita,* "not two." We are One. The same Spirit. The same Source. Everywhere. All the time.

When you see something else, hear something else, understand something else—that is divided, finite consciousness. When you see nothing else, hear nothing else, understand nothing else—that is superconsciousness.

# Everything Is an Illusion

IN THE MOUNTAINS OF HIMAREST, there once lived a monk who had become famous for his discourses on the nature of the universe. He preached that everything in the world is Maya, an illusion stemming from our state of mind.

One morning, he entered the meditation room where his disciples were waiting and sat on the straw mat. A lingering scorpion then stung him and he jumped up with a loud ouch.

One of the pupils was astonished and disappointed at the reaction since he regarded the Guru as living Buddha consciousness. He asked the monk why he felt the pain when the scorpion and the sting were all illusory.

"And so was my ouch" replied the monk.

∞

Is the universe a grand illusion, a mere antic of the mind? A shadow of reality?

We live in a virtual world. The computer age presents us with countless alternate universes with a sleight of hand.

What is your world-view? A bat without eyes is not blind, but it has a different view of the flower that it pollinates than we do.

# Om… Aum

A STUDENT OF THE SPIRIT sought to unveil the mysteries of the mantra Om. He had heard of Sage Omkar who devoted his lifetime contemplating Om. So the seeker set out on a pilgrimage to the Sage's Ashram in Omsville, nestled high up in the northern mountains. After many a night and day, he reached the Ashram and announced to the sage that he wanted to be his student. The sage took him in as his disciple and promised to reveal the secrets of Om over the following four seasons. During this time, the disciple could live as Brahmacharya, practicing chastity and austerity.

One morning, at the end of monsoon season, the sage called in the disciple and revealed to him that Om has three manifestations or states. The first is the awake state, when one is aware of external objects and experiences pleasure and pain through the sense organs. This is the relative world of subjects and objects, me and you, a dualistic world of divisions.

During autumn, the sage revealed the second manifestation of Om, the dream state when one is conscious of images. The mind flies away in all directions like a kite in the wind.

"The third aspect of Om is the deep sleep state," declared the sage after nine full moons had passed. "The mind eventually settles back into self, like the kite tethered to a rock, like the rivers that fuse with the ocean and find peace. One is freed of all effort because there are no desires, no striving of any kind."

Finally the Sage revealed that the whole Om is none other than Brahman—the Source of the mortal and the immortal, the human and the divine, the finite and the infinite—the sum and substance of supreme consciousness.

$$\infty$$

Om, the condensed form of Aum, is a trinity of three sounds: a-u-m. Each sound is a state of consciousness: "a" waking state; "u" dreaming state; "m" deep sleep state.

The whole sound as one continuous vibration is cosmic consciousness. It is a synthesis of the three universal qualities of creation, preservation, and dissolution. Om is of course the first syllable of omniscient, omnipresent, and omnipotent.

When you recite the "Ah" sound, you open the mouth wide and invite the whole universe to come in; the "Ah" is a primordial Sattvic sound. With the Rajasic "Um" sound, you close the mouth swallowing the universe. The inner space within you merges with the cosmic space. Thus you become one with Brahman.

Om… Om… Aum…

# Prana and the Chakras— Cosmic Life Force

A LONG TIME AGO the organs of perception and action got into an argument over who was the most excellent among them. The ears said they were greater than the eyes because, unlike the eyes, they were always open to the world. The eyes said they were greater because they could see farther than the ears could hear. The mind said it was the greatest because it could imagine anything whatsoever and could even travel faster than light. The arguments continued night after day.

Finally they all called on God to settle the argument: "A thousand Salutations to you, O Mighty One, pray tell us who is the greatest among us." He said: "One among you by whose absence the body suffers the most is the most excellent."

The ears departed and returned after a year and asked, "Could you live without us?" The others said: "We lived like deaf people without hearing, living through the vital breath, seeing through the eyes, speaking through the organs of speech, knowing through the mind, and procreating through the organs of generation."

Then the eyes went and returned after a year and asked: "Have you been able to live without us?" The other organs responded: "We lived like blind people without seeing, living through the vital breath, speaking through the organs of speech, knowing through the mind, and procreating through the organs of generation."

One by one, all the others took their turns and discovered that they were valuable but not indispensable. Finally, it was the turn of the vital breath. As it was about to depart, all the organs pleaded with it not to go: "Venerable Prana, none of us can survive without your energy, as a shadow cannot exist independent of the body. You are the vital breath—the spirit—that links us to the universe. You are indeed the most excellent of us all."

∞

One takes in breath just after birth and gives out breath just before death.

Breath is the spirit that unites the body, mind, and speech. By modulating your breath and breathing, you can invigorate your energy flows, your thoughts, and your health.

Breath is the life-force *Prana* that connects the finite Earth with the infinite Sky—the internal energy centers with their cosmic counterparts. Prana flows up and down subtle channels along seven *Chakras*, wheels or centers of psychic energy, energizing the whole being. You feel lethargic and unbalanced when the energy channels are blocked.

The seven Chakras are the seven planes of consciousness. Six are situated in the nerve plexuses along the spine within the physical body. The seventh and the highest Chakra is at the crown center, just above the head in the astral plane. It is the center of centers, the universal vertex of superconsciousness.

The lower Chakras are associated with creation or *Brahma;* the middle Chakras with sustenance or *Vishnu;* the higher Chakras with dissolution and renewal or *Shiva.*

Every person is centered in one of the Chakras where his thoughts and actions are concentrated. The first Chakra, at the base of the spine, is related to security and earthly survival. Also situated nearby is *Kundalini,* dormant primordial energy depicted as a slumbering serpent with magical powers. The second Chakra, near the genital area, is related to sensual pleasures and reproduction. The third near the navel is related to power and control. The consciousness of most people is centered in these three Chakras. They are the focal points of worldly endeavors.

The fourth Chakra, in the heart region, is the center of love and compassion—and of abundance. It is a bridge from the physical to the spiritual. The fifth Chakra, in the throat region, is the locus of creative and spiritual pursuits. The sixth Chakra is between and behind the eyebrows of the *third eye* in the pineal gland area. Also called the *mind's eye or inner eye,* it is the seat of intuition, the sixth sense. This inner eye transcends the bounds of time and space and reason. Some people wear a dot on the forehead as a constant reminder of this hidden faculty.

Where are you centered? Life is a little like a six-story brownstone: one can choose to spend most of the time in the penthouse or in the basement. You can strengthen the higher Chakras and Sattva qualities through the right foods and thoughts, and keeping Good Company.

Every time you have a thought or perform an action, the corresponding Chakra takes hold. For instance, when you perform a compassionate act, the heart Chakra is reinforced. This is similar to what happens in the brain when you think, see, visualize, speak, or act out something;

the corresponding region of the brain is enlarged. In other words, whatever you dwell on is strengthened in you, both the positive and the negative.

The secret of Prana is the breath. Certain breathing practices, *Pranayama*, strengthen specific Chakras and restore energy balance. Breathing deeply while focusing on the navel will strengthen the lower and the middle Chakras and the Rajas energy. Reciting the Mantra *Om* while focusing on the third eye in the forehead will strengthen the sixth wisdom Chakra and facilitate the rise of Kundalini from the dormant base to the astral plane.

Deep meditation and yoga breathing practices are essential to connecting with the universal life-force. It is like plugging in to God to recharge your cosmic batteries.

# Karma:
# Trajectory–Not Destiny

*Sow a thought, reap an action*
*Sow an action, reap a habit*
*Sow a habit, reap a character*
*Sow a character, reap a destiny.*

Samuel Smiles, *Life and Labor*

# Karma or Tamas?

ON THE BANK OF MIGHTY RIVER lived a man named Sloth. He had great faith in God and Karma. During one exuberant monsoon, there was an incessant downpour and the river started to swell and overflow its banks. Radio warnings were broadcast for people living near the river to vacate the area. Sloth ignored the warnings.

The waters continued to rise and inundated the first floor of Sloth's home. Rescue workers on boats came by, but Sloth was adamant and refused to move. He argued, "If it is God's will and if it is my Karma to die from this flood, so be it."

The water level continued to rise.

∞

Karma is neither fate nor destiny. It is predisposition, trajectory.

Karma, meaning act or deed, is not passive but active. Individuals have to work out their Karma through physical actions and experiences.

Some take refuge in the notion that Karma is a fatalistic doctrine, believing that their fate is foreordained, that it makes no difference what a person thinks or does—his fate is sealed. What Karma really proclaims is determinism, the natural law of cause-and-effect. To every action there is a reaction. "As a man sows, so shall he reap." Thus, Karma is both a deed and an effect because one reaps the harvest from Karmic seeds in due season.

Everyone is born with genetic and Karmic blueprints. They predispose a person toward certain tendencies at birth. But you can modify their initial influence through your own free will and actions. In this way, genetic and karmic heritage becomes less and less deterministic as you journey through life. Thus, neither genetic nor Karmic inheritance mandates specific results, just as a card player dealt a set of cards can play numerous ways.

There are many levels of Karma: personal, family, society, national, global, and universal. Personal Karma is three-fold: total accumulated Karma from past lives to be resolved, Karma to be experienced in this lifetime, and the Karma we are now creating. This last one is particularly important because we have better control over present actions.

Remember, then, Karma is not a sin or punishment. It is a learning experience and an evolutionary opportunity by which one can alter one's Karmic trajectory.

If you want to know your past, look at your present position. If you want to know your future, look into your present actions.

# Karma and Free Will

DAY AFTER DAY, year after year, God received blame for all the misery in the world. He seldom received credit for anything. More than a little annoyed at all the negative publicity, He convened an assembly of people's representatives.

He asked them to choose once and for all what they really wanted: "I can decide all your actions and your fate. Or you can decide and act out according to your own free will and be shepherds of your own destiny."

The representatives voted unanimously.

∞

The human spirit is endowed with something extraordinary—free will and a sense of humor. Yes, a sense of humor is what distinguishes us from God. It's the price the Absolute pays for his omniscience.

Karma cannot exist without free will. Will that is subject to habit is mechanical will. Will that is governed by spontaneity is pristine will. Will that is attuned to the spirit is divine will.

Karma releases us from the constant speculation, remorse, and blame when things seem to go wrong. We all look back occasionally and dwell on what could have been, might have been, should have been, and so on. Acceptance of the Karmic law serves as an antidote if one is discouraged by failures and suffering so far in present life—not to be a prisoner of the past, take courage in the thought that this is part of an eternal life, that one is working out past Karma and helping others in the process.

The Karmas of different people—families and friends and others—do intermingle. But each individual must work out his or her own Karma through thoughts, words, and deeds. Even though certain spiritual beings do have the power to vacate your Karma, they would not ordinarily do so because that would interfere with free will and the course of evolution.

Thus Karma serves as a relief valve—to draw lessons from the past, accept the present as is, and concentrate energies on shaping the future.

As you are the product of your past, so can you be the architect of your future.

# Faith and Ignorance

CITIZENS OF DISTANTLAND long believed that the waters of Ganga descended from heaven and were blessed with the magical power to purify all sins. Ancient lore had it that her holy waters would extinguish all fires of Karma. After completing their family duties, or whenever the opportunity arose, Distantlanders would journey to the river and perform ablutions.

One day, as pilgrims emerged from the cleansing waters, they encountered a sickly leper and his wife on the bank of the river. The wife beseeched the pilgrims, who had just been purified by Ganga, to save her husband. She begged, "Oh pure ones, free of all sins, please sprinkle a few drops of Ganga water on my husband, and lift him from Karmic suffering." She cautioned that if the person were not free of all sins, then the sprinkle would kill her husband instantly.

While they sympathized with her plight, the pilgrims didn't want to risk hastening her husband's death. But one woman—a prostitute by profession—came forward without hesitation and sprinkled Ganga on him.

She was too ignorant to question the power of Ganga.

∞

A person purifies himself through faith and action.

You do not inherit Karma from your actions alone. The past, present, and future of humanity are entwined in a thousand ways. Karmic heritage comes from one's past actions and the actions of ancestors and others. What makes Karma such a powerful force is that Karmic effects—both positive and negative—are instantaneous as well as intergenerational. As it has been said: The sins of the father are visited on the sons for seven generations.

Karma is as inevitable as it is alterable. How to partake of it? Think of each day and every event as an opportunity to lighten the old Karmic debt and build up a happy future. Every time you face a fork in the road, if you choose the right path and act positively, it will add to the positive reserves—like a deposit in a bank.

We can perform many kinds of Karmic action. Daily practices like meditation and prayer deepen self-awareness. Periodic rituals such as offering of food to animals and plants help us empathize with creatures in various stages of evolution. Ancestral death anniversary rituals connect us with the wisdom and blessings of our ancestors. Spiritual pilgrimages bring additional revelations. Performance of one's duty that is not desire-driven, as in *Karma Yoga*, is a powerful force that alters Karma trajectory.

# Life in Death: Momentous Moments of Transition

*Go, my breath, to the immortal Breath.*
*Then may this body end in ashes!*
*Remember, O my mind, the deeds of the*
*past, remember the deeds...*

*Yajur Veda*

# A Time to Die

IN THE ANCIENT KINGDOM OF GYANALAND, the noble king Gyana ruled with great wisdom and compassion. Once a week, he would receive the citizens in his court and listen to their aspirations and concerns.

One day, a wailing mother came to him carrying her child who had just died. She begged the king to bring him back to life. The king agreed to revive him but said he needed a fistful of rice from a household that had never experienced death.

She left the king assuring him she would be back soon with the rice. She went to a nearby home and begged for some rice, which she readily received. But upon further inquiry she learned there had been a death in that family a few months before. She continued door to door in search of a family that death had not visited, all to no avail.

The meaning of the king's message slowly dawned on her.

∞

The dance of life and death is one of nature's enduring cycles or spirals of continuity. One steps from the universal space into the individual space of this world at birth, and back into the universal space at death.

Everyone wonders what happens after death. Why should it be any more surprising to be born, say, a thousand times than to be born for the first time and only once?

As the body sheds worn-out garments, so does the *Indweller* shed its bodies. The physical body merges with the elements, the subtle body merges with nature, the subtlest self goes back to its Source.

It is curious that everyone wants to go to heaven but no one wants to die! Something so natural and inevitable is viewed as an anomaly, a sign of human frailty, something to be avoided at all costs. It is the paradox of man wanting to live forever but believing that death is the end of it all. It may be ego's resistance to end its separate existence. Perhaps it is the fear of the "day of judgment," fear of the unknown. Certainly it is because we forget our true origins.

While death is certain, the uncertainty is in when and how. What we all want is freedom from the fear of death, to die in peace and without regret. One cannot die peacefully if he lives a life of greed, attachment, and fear. To die well, one must live well. The first step is to recognize the inevitable connection between life and death, and life after life.

Whatever thought one has before going to sleep, one wakes up with a similar thought, consciously or unconsciously. Whatever one remembers before departing his body, he will realize hereafter, for that is what his mind and heart most dwelt on in his lifetime.

The dying help the living gain new insights and start anew. To counter the power of death, expect it at any time. To a prepared mind, death is but a crossing of the threshold to another world, one that holds tantalizing possibilities.

You have come into this world crying while others rejoiced. Leave with a smile while the others cry.

# What Is Real and What Is a Dream?

THERE ONCE LIVED GOLDSMITHS in Dreamtown. A son was born to them after several years of marriage and prayers. Goldsmith and his wife regarded their son as a precious gift from heaven and raised him with great love and reverence.

One day, as he turned five, the boy fell ill and died suddenly. The family was grief-stricken and the mother cried incessantly. Nonetheless, the father went to work the next day and returned in the evening as if nothing had happened.

Goldsmith's wife was outraged at his nonchalance and scolded him for being a heartless father, not shedding even one tear for their dead son. He replied calmly: "I had a dream last night that I became the King of this land, and had three sons. I ruled happily with the three sons until I woke up. Should I grieve for the loss of one son, or for the three sons and the kingdom?"

∞

Aren't our dreams fashioned by our worlds? We dwell in parallel universes—in a *metaverse*—with several dimensions.

Since death is both certain and unpredictable, one can accept its inevitability and choose to ignore death, assuming that not much can be done about it. Or one can take a moment to reflect on death and be prepared for it, as one cooks food before feeling hungry.

Reflection on death during moments of introspection deepens a sense of renunciation. Letting go of possessions brings freedom. The knowledge of eternal self lets us see death as a comma, not as a period.

The thresholds between present life, death, and rebirth are momentous occasions. What you are and what you dwell on at the end of your present life sets in motion a momentum that is carried forward into the beginning of next life. If you go to bed at night with peaceful thoughts, you will have pleasant dreams. But if you go to sleep angry and agitated, are you not likely to get nightmares?

The moments before death, the *bardos*, present an exceptional window to lighten Karma. They straddle two worlds, the world one is leaving and the world one is entering. Pious and peaceful thoughts at the threshold shape the future.

The atmosphere around a dying person should inspire positive emotions of compassion, peace, and detachment. He can fill the mind with memories of meritorious deeds and favorite deities. A virtuous state of mind at death brings about virtuous rebirth.

You may prepare a brief passage or a few phrases to say to the dying and help them die in freedom and dignity. And prepare something for yourself to recall—perhaps your good deeds and personal deity.

A person departing from this world has three kinds of friends to accompany him. His wealth says goodbye from home. His family and friends come to the burial grounds. His good deeds follow him everywhere.

# Reincarnation and Nirvana

ONCE UPON A TIME, the legendary king of Himaland ruled in peace and prosperity with his two queens. Each queen had a son, one named Durya and the other Arju. On the eve of his 75th birthday, the king announced that he would bequeath the kingdom to his two sons and retire to the mountains.

Prince Durya coveted the whole kingdom. Knowing his brother's weakness for adventure, Durya devised a devious scheme and challenged Arju to a game of checkers. Whoever lost the game would have to leave the palace and spend ten years in a forest incognito. If, during this time, the prince's identity were disclosed, the ten year exile would start all over again. The stage was set and the game began with much fanfare. Durya played with loaded dice and won. Although Arju realized what had happened, he accepted his defeat and disappeared into the forest.

After leading an austere life incognito for ten years, Arju returned to the palace and claimed his half of the kingdom. But Prince Durya, who had become the king, refused to share any part of the kingdom. When Arju pleaded for an estate of a few villages, Durya would not yield even an inch. A battle between the forces of the two had become inevitable.

The opposing armies of the two brothers were arrayed against each other poised to fight. Surveying the battlefield and seeing his relatives, friends and teachers on the other side, Arju began to have second thoughts. He pondered whether the kingdom was worth the carnage and grief that the battle would surely bring. His determination began to waver.

Arju's chariot was being piloted by his revered guru and mentor. The omniscient Charioteer discerned the conflicts in Arju's mind and explained the nature of the mortal body and the immortal soul, the nature of free will and Dharma, the nature of action and results, and the nature of reincarnation and Nirvana.

He counseled and enlightened the beleaguered Arju thus: "As a Kshatriya prince, it is your duty, Dharma, to protect your kingdom and honor regardless of the consequences. Action can either bind you to this world or liberate you from it. If you die in fulfillment of your duty, it will only hasten the moment of reunion with the immortal Self, your Nirvana. Birth and death are earthly accompaniments of life. That which is, shall never cease to be. As to your brother and his entourage, they too are working out their Karma and, through reincarnation, will soon merge with the eternal spirit."

∞

Action is the essence of creation and the crux of Karma. Actions, both good and bad, biased with expectations of results, accumulate Karma and are binding. Actions performed in fulfillment of one's Dharma incur no Karma and are liberating.

Reincarnations—birth, death, and rebirth—are but stations in our journey toward final destiny. Human consciousness is like information or energy that can't be destroyed but only transmuted. Consciousness is capsulated in a succession of forms imprinted by *Karma.* Unfulfilled desires also bind one to the Karmic Wheel of Reincarnation. The self moves on from one habitat to another, evolving through reincarnation until all Karmas are resolved.

Why then don't we remember past lives? Why do we have particular affinities—to mathematics or music, for example, or to certain places and people? Is it all by chance? But imagine the confusion it would cause if you knew, for instance, the hundreds of mothers and fathers you have had in past lives, to whom you might have been a parent.

But some people, child prodigies and others, are able to remain connected through reawakened memories of their past and build on foundations that have already been laid. It may be that as Karma plays out, most people don't remember details of their past lives because that would hinder free will and hold back spiritual progress.

Virtuous rebirths, desirable as they may be, are still subject to the law of Karma. The other path is a *path of no return, Nirvana.* When one abides in the infinite spirit, one transcends the wheel of birth and death and climbs the heights of union with the immortal Self.

# Proprietors or Participants?

*Earth gives enough to satisfy everyone's need but not everyone's greed.*

Mahatma Gandhi

# Sure Sounds
# Like a Hotel!

AFTER WALKING MANY A MILE, a monk on a pilgrimage arrived at a village late at night. He needed to rest for the night so that he could continue his journey in the morning. He knocked on the door of a house with walls adorned by portraits of spiritual icons. When the door was opened, the monk requested shelter for the night.

The householder was angered at being disturbed in the middle of the night, and exclaimed that this was not a hotel. The monk asked who lived in the house before him. "My uncle." "Who lived here before your uncle?" "A family that moved to the city." "Who owns the house now?" persisted the monk. "I and a money lender," said the householder with much annoyance.

"It sure sounds like a hotel to me," intoned the monk.

∞

All the real estate rights we have on this planet are "squatters rights."

A bird has all the sky it needs to fly. No bird ever ran out of sky.

A momentous leap occurs with the realization that one has nothing of his own, yet one has everything. When you give it all up, you have it all.

Such transformation begins when you share what you consider valuable with a widening circle—people close to you, then those for whom you have no particular feelings, finally people whom you may not like.

# Who Should
# be Thankful?

THE MONK AND PHILOSOPHER VIVEK visited Utopica a century ago and gave a series of lectures on religion, duties, and stewardship. He met with several prominent citizens. One of them, Mr. Richfeller, was at first reluctant to visit the monk but was persuaded by his friends to call on him.

Upon learning of the vast riches of Richfeller, Vivek asked him what he was doing with the wealth bestowed on him and enjoined him to put it to good use. Annoyed by this gratuitous advice, Richfeller walked out.

But he returned to the monk a few days later and said that he had given away most of his money to charity so the monk should now be happy and thankful. To which the monk responded, "On the contrary, it is you who should be thankful."

∞

Few people have such a rare opportunity to raise societal Sattva and lighten their Karma.

When you give out your best, you bring out your best.

People often confuse the roles of owner, controller, and trustee. One can claim ownership for a time. Man's dominion over fellow men and things is only temporary.

All of one's possessions will be taken away some day. One should remember what one can take to the next world.

We don't inherit the earth, we borrow it from our children.

# The Nurture of Nature

*Understand the thrust of the yang…*
*But be more like the yin in your being*
*Be like a valley — that parts to its stream*
*Be like a stream…*
*And channel it — so it flows to the sea*
*— Lao Tzu, Tao Te Ching*

# The Benefactor Who Was Refused Entry to Heaven

A WELL-KNOWN BENEFACTOR died and was on his way to heaven when he was stopped at the gate. He was baffled since he had performed numerous noble deeds to uplift humanity. But said the gatekeeper by the name of Atmosphere, "All your life, you took in good air and put out bad air with carbon dioxide and various other pollutants." So it was that he was sent back as a tree for a hundred years to restore air quality.

After serving as a tree, the Benefactor again appeared at the heavenly gate and was again rebuffed. A new gatekeeper named Water said that all his life the Benefactor had used quality water and put out degraded water. Consequently, he had to go back to earth as ultraviolet light to destroy microbial contaminants and improve water quality.

After paying his dues as a tree and ultraviolet light, he appeared again at the heavenly gate. "Not so fast" said Land, another gatekeeper. "All your life you used and threw away so many things that poisoned the land. Go back as an earthworm to make at least partial amends."

∞

We are nature—born of stars and skies, water and wind—ever changing, ever the same. Night follows day, tides rise and fall, seasons come and go.

The universal elements of air, water, fire, earth, and space—of which our bodies are fashioned—are given to us freely by nature. We didn't create them. We don't own them.

Nature is a reflection of the cosmic order. It has neither motive nor purpose. It is neither good nor bad. It is perfect simply being what it is.

Mother nature is all-embracing—it rains without judgment on trees and weeds, on mountains and oceans.

The nature of nature—the rhythms, the unity, the diversity, the symmetry, the asymmetry—resonates deep within us and in all creation. Some of nature's manifestations—plants and trees, rivers and oceans, minerals and fuels—are the real bottom line of all life: food and medicine, wealth and esthetics. Our environment is where we live, love, and play.

Nature evokes mixed feelings of harmony, fear, awe. When we are in sync with nature, we are in harmony with ourselves. Early man reacted with fear at such events as floods and drought. Later he prayed for rains and bountiful harvest. He marveled at nature's power over life and death. Throughout, the *yin-yang* of nature has been a soother of souls and the fountain of inspiration. Mountain peaks heighten our Sattva quality; wilderness connects us with our primal nature to wander free.

In the relentless march of civilization, human success depended not only on how we fit into nature, our adaptation, but also how we made nature fit us. Human ecological footprints have extended to the far corners of the Earth. Our ability to transform our external environment has far outpaced our ability to transform our inner nature—from being a conqueror to being a citizen of the natural world. Nature is yet to be our second nature.

As an astronaut on spaceship Earth, what is your true habitat? Is it the space you occupy, the home you live in, this planet, the solar system, the milky way galaxy, or this universe?

# Everything Connected

SOME TIME AGO, there was a raging malaria epidemic in Mosquitoland. A pesticide was sprayed extensively to eradicate the mosquitoes that carried malaria parasites. The malaria was brought under control, replaced instead by a greater calamity.

The lizards in the houses died from eating the poisoned insects and the cats died from eating the lizards. Freed from cats, the rats carrying typhus-infested fleas ran rampant.

And then, the thatched roofs in the villages started to collapse. The pesticide had also killed the wasps and other insects that ate the caterpillars that fed on the thatched roofs. The malaria problem was "solved" by typhus epidemic and crumbling houses.

∞

All the living and the non-living—we are all within each other like streams that flow in and out of the ocean. Connected in space, connected in the distant past, connected with the virtual future.

We are all different but not separate or independent, like the trunk and leaves of a tree. A tree may look distinct and separate but it has no independent existence of its own. It is a link in the vast network of subtle connections that stretch across the universe. The rain that falls on its leaves and on its roots, the air and the sunlight that enfold it, the soil that anchors and nourishes it, the means that pollinate and perpetuate it—a few of the more obvious cross-links—are all part of the tree. And we are all branches of the same tree.

Everything in the universe is like everything else, but not exactly like anything else. As we move away from our origins, from the Source, we see more and more diversity. As we move closer to the Source, we see more and more unity. Unity accords strength, diversity wealth.

Our genetic fraternity, reflected in the blueprint of all life—from single-cell microbes to humans with trillions of cells—entwines exquisite simplicity with astounding complexity. Human genes are not only an archive of human history, but of all life since the beginning. The basic cellular functions are the same—be it in paramecium, petunia, or people. But the nature of the connections does vary. Not only are the trillions of cells in a human body connected to each other, but they are also connected to the trillions and trillions of *cells* in the universe. The human body is like a *cell* in the *universal body*. Man and the environment are an integral organism. There is not one without the other.

A few ingredients of nature—space, fire, earth, water, and air—are recycled and reconfigured in endless ways. Consider air and water so central to life. We have been inhaling the same air and ingesting the same water that permeated the sinews of dinosaurs and billions of others before and since. We have been sharing the same atoms and molecules not only with other humans but with millions of other species across the globe, separated by billions of years. Matter and energy are constantly being recycled in and out of all living and nonliving phenomena. Dust to dust, ashes to ashes.

Like it or not, we are all exchanging our minds and bodies through the thoughts we think, through the air we breathe, through the energy we radiate. Everything in the universe is interacting, changing subtly, every moment.

# The Bacteria that Went on Strike

ONCE UPON A TIME, fed up with constant denigration by humans, the bacterial species held a conference in Bactorum Townhall to discuss their plight. They quickly and unanimously reached an agreement henceforward to have nothing to do with humans. All bacteria left humans and their products. Other microbial species such as fungi also joined the strike in sympathy.

It wasn't long before humans started encountering a deluge of problems in the absence of the bacteria they had taken for granted. Gastrointestinal problems were among the first to appear since bacteria no longer helped in digestion and in vitamin synthesis. Human wastes began to pile up and sewage started fouling the atmosphere. Everyday products from bread to yogurt to wine could not be made any longer in the absence of yeast.

The human race soon got the message and sent a representative to negotiate with the bacteria. The microbes agreed to return on the condition that any time they were criticized, equal time would be devoted to publicizing their beneficial and indispensable role.

∞

We owe a debt of gratitude to our simpler colleagues. Bacteria are not mean-spirited interlopers; they held title to this planet billions of years before humans

We should fight bacteria and other microbes as worthy competitors to keep them in balance, but not try to obliterate them because we are not independent of microbes. Not only that, the more we try to kill them, the stronger they become.

It so happens, there are far more bacteria in a person's mouth than the total number of people that ever walked this planet. The mouth is an ecosystem unto itself, a hidden biosphere, with the profusion and diversity reminiscent of a rain forest. A hundred trillion microbes live in or on our bodies, exceeding the number of our own cells. One might go so far as to say that human bodies are bacterial colonies, mostly living in a spirit of coexistence. Some people filter their drinking water to eliminate bacteria; others so that the bacteria may live.

Trillions of bacteria inhabit our intestinal tracts, help synthesize vitamins, stimulate the immune system, and stake out a territory excluding harmful opportunistic types. Children who were not exposed to bacteria early in life may not have developed the necessary immunity. Many disorders are caused when things go out of balance, a crossing over the border. It is not the invading microbes but the host's response that often causes the damage.

Not only do humans and bacteria share common origins, but nested in the human body are thousands of plant and bacterial relics, as well as numerous permanent and transient lodgers. Mitochondria, the energy factories inside cells that fuel life's processes, were originally bacteria that got incorporated into the cells billions of years ago. The plant chloroplasts that carry out photosynthesis had their origin in blue green algae. These chloroplasts and the mitochondria are the twin engines of life on this planet.

The microbial contribution to humanity is continuing in many fields, from cleaning up contaminated land and water to genetic engineering.

From the single-cell bacteria to humans with trillions of cells, we are all threads in the tapestry of life.

# The Serpent that Suppressed Its Nature

A CERTAIN SERPENT in a park near a village acquired a terrible reputation by hissing at everyone who passed by and biting people indiscriminately. One day, seeing a monk resting on a nearby bench, it suddenly got spiritual and approached him for advice. The monk counseled the serpent to stop biting and harassing all passersby.

The serpent faithfully followed the monk's advice. This didn't go unnoticed by the villagers. Encouraged by its meek behavior, some children even started throwing stones at it. But the serpent would not retaliate. Some time later, the monk was passing through the park again and noticed that the serpent was bruised all over and barely alive. He asked what had happened.

The serpent said that in compliance with the monk's advice, it had stopped biting and even hissing. The monk acknowledged that he did advise the snake not to bite people. "But why did you stop hissing to discourage people from causing harm?" he asked.

∞

Nature prevails, ultimately, in one form or another.

When man "suppresses" the course of nature by damming rivers, felling trees indiscriminately, and changing the global climate and earth's balance—nature "restores" the balance with devastating floods and fires, soil erosion, and diminished diversity and ecosystem wealth.

Over the millennia human nature has evolved through genetic as well as cultural inheritance. We have a genetic body and a cultural body—sculpted by the arts, the scriptures, the tools, the values. The human mind has evolved much faster than the body, creating conflicts between the biological mind and the psychosocial mind.

Why do we feel such a powerful urge to revisit our past? It is our longing to get back in touch with our primal nature, our primal source. Every one of us is a monument to our ancestors. We draw on some unconscious connections with our ancestors in who we are and what we do.

The biological patterns—our tendency to store fat, the tendency to hoard, the senses' external orientation, the fight-or-flight response, territoriality, and wanderlust—all date back to the cave-dwelling and hunting era of danger and scarcity. These tendencies served us well in the past and became crystallized in the human psyche, conferring certain evolutionary advantages for the "selfish" genes to perpetuate themselves.

Coupled with these biological antecedents of scarcity and competition was also the powerful urge for cooperation and compassion. Man's dual nature from the evolutionary fabric, the mismatch between man's primal tendencies and the new social order, strains the balance between man and society.

Such is the nature of Nature.

# Of Wellness and Disease

*Hidden in the mystery of consciousness*
*the mind, incorporeal, flies alone far away...*
*the practice of the highest consciousness —*
*this is teaching of the Buddha...*

— *Dhammapada*

# The Merchant's
# Mysterious Illness

ONCE THERE WAS A WEALTHY MERCHANT who had come to suffer great agony. He could not sleep at all. He visited many famous doctors and medical centers. After comprehensive examinations and scores of tests, they all pronounced him perfectly healthy. Yet he continued to be tormented by the mysterious affliction.

Finally, he was referred to an unorthodox practitioner who specialized in obscure illnesses. The merchant went to see the doctor with volumes of medical records and test results. The doctor set them aside and, looking deep into the merchant's eyes, asked him what his occupation was. The merchant balked at the question and asked the doctor to concentrate instead on his medical information.

But the doctor persisted and the man told him he was a merchant. The doctor said that if the merchant wanted to be his patient, he would be locked up in a room and would be required to make a list of all the wrongs he had committed in his occupation before he was allowed to leave. The merchant thought the doctor was a charlatan, but yielded to the peculiar demand—anything to rid himself of his affliction.

The merchant was taken to an isolated room. An hour later he emerged with a long list. He admitted he was actually a narcotics dealer, making huge profits in the illegal trade. The doctor advised him to change his occupation at once and to devote his accumulated wealth to improving community health. He suggested that the merchant see him again in six months.

Not more than a month passed before the merchant called the doctor and said he had been following the doctor's prescription. He was feeling much better and did not expect to have to see the doctor again.

∞

There are three types of illnesses. Physical illness is caused by the accumulation of chemical and biological toxins. Mental and emotional sickness results from the accumulation of mental debris—anger, fear, greed, remorse, jealousy, hatred. Spiritual sickness is due to ignorance of self.

We are in the best of health not just when we are not ill, but when we feel unbounded, creative, and joyous, befitting our primal nature.

Consciousness is the master key to wellness and disease. The purer the consciousness, the more powerful its expressions. Our conscious and subconscious messages percolate deep into every cell and orchestrate the physiology and anatomy. Your body is a facsimile of your thoughts. The mind is not in your body, the body is in your mind.

People can become more mindful of all that they take into their bodies and minds. With all the noise in the name of information in modern societies, the access and control of one's mind is unwittingly passed on to some unknown characters. Information is a double-edged sword—it can be enlightening or polluting, enabling or disabling.

Constant exposure to sense objects multiplies desires. Attachment to desires causes anxiety and confusion. Confusion obscures understanding. Where is peace without understanding, and where is joy without peace?

Daily life is full of conflicts and fears. Many fears arise and grow as one can mistake a rope for a snake in darkness. The world of imaginary snakes can become overwhelming unless one turns on the light and sees the rope for what it is.

This is not to say that real causes of suffering do not exist. How does one cope with suffering, for example, from disease, old age, and tragedies that are the inevitable accompaniments of life?

Looking at a situation as an observer, as a detached witness, will allow space to accept suffering as a natural part of life, not without purpose. Distress may be a sign from inside that you are moving away from your self and that you need to pause and change course.

Hatred is for the weak, compassion is for the strong. Some ask "why me?" while others ask "why not me?" Thinking like a victim can bring momentary solace, attention, and sympathy, but will only reinforce negative states of mind. Adversity could help the roots go deeper to seek nourishment and strength from hidden sources.

Hate, anger, fear, guilt, jealousy—these are internal enemies. They eat up Sattva if you cling to them. Thoughts acquire power only if you pay attention. Decide, if you so wish, not to entertain feelings of unhappiness for more than, say, 10 seconds. You can also void a negative thought before it goes too far—before it leaves an imprint—by taking a deep breath and recalling a personal mantra, deity, or some other affirmation. But even anger can sometimes prove to be a positive emotion if it energizes you to positive action.

Most people are concerned about external hygiene but overlook internal hygiene. The seeds of negative thoughts, once implanted in the mind, grow insidiously even in sleep and result in tremendous stores of negative energy. Just as you purge physical wastes from your body daily, so should you flush out and purge toxic thoughts from your mind, sweep away the mental debris from inner citadels. Meditation, focusing on breath, serves as an internal vacuum cleaner to sweep off negative emotions.

You cannot always control others' behavior, but you can control your own response. A negative person or situation will pass. Think of the other person as another "you" at another time. Connect with the other person's consciousness and try to see something of yourself. If a person is evoking strong negative emotions, turn it around into positive feelings by praying for him or her to receive God's guidance. This is not to condone unfair behavior; sometimes the right thing to do is to firmly counter such behavior.

Happiness dwells in both realms of our existence, symbolized by the heart and the mind. The heart with its predilection for continuity, constancy, and ceremony; the mind thriving on change, mystery, and adventure. Stillness and constancy, movement and change—these are the bricks and mortar of a tranquil home—an inner sanctuary, like the stillness of deep ocean unruffled by surface turbulence.

When your physical, mental, and spiritual beings come into harmony, you will uncover new energy reserves. But that doesn't mean you can neglect sleep. You can live with little food and shelter, but not without rest. In deep sleep, you rest in the depths of self, free of ego, free from all striving, free of the usual limitations of time, space, and form. Everyone becomes a yogi in deep sleep.

It is well to set aside some time every day to commune with nature and works of beauty—music, art, poetry, an orchid, a spiritual person. Regard it as your daily dose of spiritual vitamins.

Practice the highest consciousness—right thoughts, right speech, right deeds. Right livelihood.

# The Doctor
# Who Was More

A DOCTOR well-loved and respected in Healthville was retiring from public health service. The position was advertised and attracted a number of candidates. Three were called for an interview. They all came at the appointed time and sat in the waiting room. The retiring doctor who was to interview them walked in two hours late.

The first candidate was called in, shown a glass of water three-quarters full, and was asked what it meant. Already annoyed at the delay, he muttered something about the glass being half-empty versus half-full, pessimism and optimism. The interviewer then pointed to a tree in the backyard that was shedding leaves and asked the candidate what he thought of the tree. The candidate said it represented the various seasons. Finally, he was asked to explain why he was asked the first two questions. He said he didn't know and wondered aloud what all these had to do with medicine.

The second candidate more or less repeated what the first candidate said.

The third candidate said that the less-than-full glass depicted a human condition, perhaps immunity, which was less than optimal at the time, and needed to be restored. And the bare tree, he said, represented natural rhythms that all living entities go through, the four seasons representing the four stages in a person's life.

To the third question, he responded that although questions from patients may not seem medically relevant, a good doctor would show patience and understanding in responding to patients' concerns. He admitted that he was annoyed at being made to wait more than two hours, and understood that the delay had probably been deliberate. He added that he recognized the need to develop greater sensitivity to the concerns of patients who often had to wait a long time to see a doctor. Thus he became the clear choice to replace the beloved retiring doctor.

∞

The art of healing blends the physical, the mental, and the spiritual in a holistic way to restore natural balance.

The focus of modern medicine has come to be on disease, based on the notion that the body is like a machine that can be repaired when it breaks down, and that the problem of disease can be solved by destroying the predator, microbes or some other villain. This kind of insular approach had unraveled many a natural ecosystem. Yet the same model is applied to treat human health with the belief that human beings are housed in solid, independent bodies.

Actually, the body, mind, and spirit comprise a complex ecology, a landscape with an open fence—or like a river, flowing, replenishing, renewing. Just as the quality and the course of a river change with the waters flowing in and out of the terrain it traverses, the terrain of consciousness—our mental states—influence the course of our health and well-being.

The right consciousness is a superb formulary, the best healer within. Many ailments are self-limiting and correct themselves, if you let them.

Laughter is indeed the best medicine. It's the eruption of the spirit. But the Spirit can only laugh through the wherewithal of your body, mind, and heart.

# The Capricious Food

ON THE OCCASION of annual penance, a merchant invited a yogi wandering through the village square to a feast. The yogi readily accepted the invitation and accompanied the merchant to his home.

The merchant and his wife served him a feast with a course of seven delicacies in ornate silver dishes. The yogi was particularly attracted by a silver spoon, and the more food he ate the more attracted he became to the spoon, until finally he slipped it into his satchel.

After the meal, the likes of which he had never had, the yogi thanked his host and continued his journey. On the way, he felt tired and sought shelter under a banyan tree from the midafternoon sun. Soon he felt sick and threw up all the food.

Once purged of the food, which had affected his thinking and actions, the yogi became aware of the wrong he had committed. He hurried back to the merchant's home and returned the spoon. He begged for forgiveness and pleaded that he be allowed to serve them and redeem himself.

The merchant implored the yogi to take him as his disciple for a day. He then followed in the yogi's footsteps to the outskirts of the village.

Thus was the beginning of a long journey of an illustrious disciple.

∞

All creatures are made of food, and to food they return. The coarsest part of food becomes waste, the medium becomes flesh, the subtlest becomes the mind.

Choosing the right foods is important for purifying the body and the mind. The food we eat, the water we drink, the air we breathe—all energize the body, the mind and the spirit.

Sattva foods include water, fresh vegetables, beans, herbs, nuts. and other natural foods. Rajas spicy foods, meats and sweets. Tamas meats, alcohol and drugs.

Pause a second before and after eating. Take a sip of water before eating to clothe the naked food with a primal source. Know what you eat, eat what you like, taste what you eat. When you really taste the food, much is revealed. Also think of variety, moderation, and balance.

Just as important as the quality of the food is the quality of the company—the fellowship of noble people and places, and shared activity of families and friends.

The value of nutrition, work, and all endeavors can be enhanced by aligning with biorhythms and the diurnal cycles of light and dark, the rhythms of nature. Artificial light from electricity has been around only for a century or so. Our biological clocks have been ticking to the rhythms of the sun and the moon for millions of years.

With food, less can be more. One may fast periodically to cleanse the body and give rest to the organs and habits. To fast, Upavas, is to be "near God." Now and then, you may also want to interrupt the habit of speaking. It will be the day of rest.

Food has become a habit rather than a resource. Which is why it is good to occasionally think about what the food consists of and where it came from; the people who grew and harvested the food; and those who transported and cooked and served the food. Also involved are the thousands in the manufacture and distribution of the various tools, the housing, the pots and pans, the fuel, and so on. Acknowledge as well nature's gift of sun and rain that made it all possible.

If you wish to abstain from certain foods such as meats, let go of the thought as well as the food. Desires denied acquire lives of their own.

Changes in food habits and agricultural practices will improve not only natural resource efficiency of the food chain but also our health and environmental quality.

Good food is a staple of Sattva. These can also raise Sattva levels: service, mindfulness, meditation, love, scriptures, sacred spaces, holy men, music, works of beauty, good company, nature, stars, humor.

# Beyond Knowledge and Wisdom

*A certain wise man*
*in search of immortality...*
*turned his sight inward*
*and saw the self within*

—Katha Upanishad

# The Donkey's
# Imaginary Shackles

THERE WAS A WASHERMAN in a village who collected peoples' dirty clothes every day on a donkey and took them to the river for washing. One day he fell sick and asked his son to take the clothes for washing. The son welcomed the chance to skip school and spend a day by the river.

But when the son tried to take out the donkey, it wouldn't budge an inch. After trying different ways to persuade the donkey to move, he went into the house and told his father that the donkey refused to move even though it wasn't tied to anything.

Said the father: "I forgot to tell you something. I touch the donkey's legs with a rope and pretend to tie it to a tree at night so it won't wander away. You have to pretend to untie the donkey in the morning."

∞

Why does the mind keep missing the obvious?

The original mind is open, whole, and spontaneous. But when the mind is filled with preconceptions, it becomes a partial mind.

A donkey laden with gold only knows its weight, not its value.

How does the knower know? One way of knowing is through direct observation using the body's inlet senses. Another way is by inference with the intellect, which lies just beyond direct experience. We knew the Earth was round long before the photographs from space satellites. Reasoning takes time and requires proof.

Knowledge is revealed through science as well as faith. In science we look for uncertainty. In faith we look for certainty. In science, we look to explanations; in faith to revelations. What is known through science, awesome as it is, is minuscule compared to what is to be known.

Most everyday knowledge is acquired through experience. One learns and remembers through both the mental body and the emotional body. What is received and how it is remembered is colored by one's state of mind. Emotions interfere with perception. We tend to see things not as they are but as we are. Sattva is the right state for learning and remembering. Memory of things received in Sattva light lasts indefinitely, retaining the original fidelity. When the first thought springs from Sattva, all subsequent thoughts are true as well. Rajas active memory will last for some time but the initial memory may become distorted. The dark Tamas observations are clouded from the start, and fade away quickly. Good sleep, like Sattva, helps memory and creativity.

Learning to learn is the way of knowledge. Genuine learning combines experience, thinking, feeling, and intuition. Learning is not merely acquiring information. Information is not knowledge. Knowledge is not wisdom. Otherwise, encyclopedias and librarians would be the most learned.

Absolute knowledge is realized by sentient beings through direct revelation.

When you come to know your self, the secret of the sages will have been revealed to you.

# Tyranny of
# Linear Thinking

THERE ONCE WAS A TRAVELING HAT SALESMAN who bicycled from village to village peddling his wares. One hot summer day, on his way to Thinkville, he stopped to rest under an expansive Banyan tree and fell asleep with his hat sack beside him.

When he woke up, he saw several monkeys dangling from the branches up above wearing his hats. Recalling what he had learned about monkey behavior, the salesman took off the hat he was wearing and threw it to the ground. The monkeys did likewise. The salesman gathered up all his hats and went on his way.

Several years later, traveling the same route, he fell asleep under the same tree. When he woke up, he again discovered that the monkeys had taken the hats from his sack. Remembering the success he had had in the past, the salesman took his hat off and threw it on the ground.

One of the monkeys snatched up the hat and ran off with it.

∞

The present is not what it used to be, for man or monkey.

The human race is addicted to linear thinking, to the notion that the future is a mere extrapolation of the past.

Sometimes, though, the past can be quite revealing since we live in a world of cycles—daily cycles, weekly cycles, business cycles, life cycles, and the like. Life itself is not a linear progression from birth to death but rather a cyclical journey.

People often think that knowledge, intelligence, thinking, creativity, and even performance are more or less equivalent—that one follows naturally and inevitably from the other. They are related to be sure, but are quite different.

Intelligence is innate potential with many faces from mathematics to music, from logic to spirit. Both nature and nurture play a role. The intelligence related to the quantity of information stored—memorized information that can be retrieved on demand—is of limited value beyond school and intelligence tests. This is especially so today, when we have instantaneous access to unlimited information at our fingertips.

Thinking directs intelligence and experience toward a goal. Intelligence is akin to the horsepower of a car, while thinking is analogous to the driving skill of the operator, or like a horse and its jockey. A skilled thinker also thinks about thinking, *metacognition*.

What about creativity? Thinking and creativity are quite different. Our left brain has a proclivity for logical thinking, the right brain for universal perception. Thinking is Rajasic, movement toward a goal, attachment to a result. Creativity is Sattvic, stillness, not attached to or limited by any preconceived goal. Creativity involves withdrawal or emptying, followed by conception or expression. Emptiness is like the *Creator* and expression is like the *creation*. As one moves from the created to the Creator, toward the empty no-thing of pure consciousness, one is drawn to the wellspring of creativity.

One of the worst blocks to creativity is addiction to logic. Another is the obsession to be always right. Experience can be the worst block of all.

# Wisdom
# Beyond Logic

ONCE UPON A TIME IN DRACONIA, a doctor, a lawyer, and a professor were condemned to die by guillotine.

The doctor volunteered to go first as he hated to be kept waiting. At the appointed time, the stage was set for beheading and the guillotine came down. But the blade stopped just an inch short of the doctor's neck. He was set free in keeping with Draconia's tradition. The same thing happened to the lawyer and they both walked away, the doctor complaining about having to return to the medical bureaucracy, the lawyer discerning an opportunity for suing the guillotine manufacturer.

When the professor's turn came, having observed the malfunction, he stopped the guillotine operator and adjusted here and there some screws and bolts.

His solution worked out perfectly.

∞

Perception is more important than analysis. Intuition is preferable to intellect. Humility should come before hubris.

Knowledge is the base of understanding. Absolute knowledge cannot be created but only perceived. The principle of gravity, for instance, was always true before humans recognized it. It would be a chaotic world indeed if it could not function without the sanction of human knowledge.

Knowledge is both absolute and relative. *Veda*, absolute knowledge, is by divine revelation. That which is "heard" is called *Shruti*. It was revealed directly to *Rishis*. On the other hand, *Smriti*, that which is "remembered," is ancillary knowledge and tradition based on human experience.

Absolute knowledge—knowledge that holds true everywhere, always—springs from the Absolute. It surfaces through certain people at certain times in certain forms as relative knowledge to meet the needs of the times. Absolute knowledge has no human authors and no boundaries. Vedas are not attributed to any particular authors, there are no copyrights. Knowledge belongs to the Absolute, not to be used for personal fame or fortune.

The revelations to *Rishis* were transmitted directly from teachers to qualified pupils for thousands of years through oral tradition. This tradition ensured close contact between teacher and student, and minimized the risk of misinterpretation and dilution.

Primal "knowledge" initially found expression through the divine arts—music, painting, dance—embodying the Hindu trinity: Brahma, Vishnu, and Shiva.

# In Quest
# of the Ultimate

A LEARNED MONK went in search of what lies beyond knowledge and came upon a Savant. The savant asked what the monk had already learned. Said the monk: "I have studied the scriptures, history and science, dialogues and monologues, all kinds of rituals, life in this world and in other worlds. What is greater than knowledge?"

"Deep Reflection," said the savant, "earth, skies, nature, are all reflecting, and what we receive are fruits of such reflection."

"Is there anything greater than deep reflection?" pursued the monk. "Perception, for only through the faculty of perception can one understand knowledge and the fruits of reflection; it is the chrysalis of wisdom and creativity," said the savant. "Is there anything greater than perception?" continued the monk. "Clearly, eternal Space," the savant responded, "because space is in everything and around everything; it witnesses everything, but is affected by nothing." "Is there anything greater than space?" the monk persisted.

"Ah," said the savant finally, "you are in quest of the Absolute: the transcendent Self. He who rejoices and revels in the Self, merges with truth, consciousness, and bliss."

∞

The essence of our being is Brahman: *Satchitananda: Sat-Chit-Anand*—truth, consciousness, bliss.

In day-to-day life, we experience waves of pleasure and pain, and troughs of despair and boredom. In this state of mind, life is perceived as a struggle. Misery is seen as real and ecstasy as unreal.

People draw a little circle around them and try to find happiness from external artifacts and relationships. This kind of happiness is not pure. It is tainted by the fear of an ending, for such happiness is seen as a prelude to some impending doom and gloom.

The true state of Humanity is pure happiness, for unhappiness cannot exist in the Self.

Why then don't we feel the bliss all the time? It is always present everywhere and available in the Sattva state. We all experience momentary lapses into ecstasy. But most of the time, the bliss is blocked by the attachments, distractions, and forgetfulness of Rajas and Tamas qualities. In order to become fully established in Sattva, one has to come back, come back, come back—again and again and again—to serve, to love, to meditate, to be Good Company.

Mankind wants four things, ultimately. We want to know everything. We want to be unconditionally happy. We want to be completely free. And we want to live forever.

Omniscient, joyous, free, and immortal is what the Self is. To that you can add nothing. From that you can subtract nothing. Of such is the kingdom of Self.

Would you like to inhabit this kingdom?

# The Business of Business: Creating Abundance

*Use capitalism to make money.*
*Use spiritualism to share the wealth.*

—Dalei Lama

# Staying in Business

THERE WAS ONCE A POPULAR MONK who expounded eloquently about rights and wrongs, riches and rags, and the virtues of renunciation. People visited him day and night to clarify all sorts of doubts. The only requirement to see him was that they bring to him a piece of fruit and a silver coin on each visit.

This went on for months. One day, a villager approached the monk and said the wise monk had resolved all his doubts except one. "Why does the monk speak so persuasively about renunciation and yet insist on a fruit and silver coin from each visitor?"

"Well," said the monk, "I have to survive long enough to go to the next village and secure a place to spread the message."

∞

What is business but the exchange of the gifts of nature and the products of knowledge?

The business of business is to find abundance, to create wealth of all kinds. Financial surplus is essential to the functioning of a business but not its purpose any more than the purpose of humans is to ingest food.

At the heart of a business enterprise are the 3Ps: People, Planet, and Profits. Business organizations are among the most powerful instruments devised by man to create individual and societal wealth. Contrary to what many believe, businesses do not flourish by creating scarcity. Unveiling abundance—through personal freedom, through the joy of discovery, through ongoing institutions—is the essence of human enterprise.

Everyone thinks of the obligations of businesses to customers and to society. What about the obligations of customers and other citizens to businesses?

In business, as in all walks of life, three functions must be performed: Creation, Preservation, Dissolution. In an ancient religion, a trinity of gods—Brahma, Vishnu, Shiva—performed these functions. In business too, we need entrepreneurs to beget new offspring, champions to nurture infants with surpluses, and dissolvers to spin off or let die moribund entities to restore potential from creative destruction.

The modern business idea of an "infinite stream" of income may well have a precedent in some age-old practices. Since ancient times, religious and spiritual ceremonies had been performed and freedom from evil forces granted, in return for a portion of crop yields in perpetuity, the beneficial effects supposedly lasting only as long as the payments were kept up. This was, indeed, an ingenious scheme to create a perpetual stream of income for religious and spiritual heads.

Business is about competition as well. Managers pay most attention to external competition, not to internal competition. Without the challenges of external competition, an organization will wither away as surely as a prey without a predator. Managing internal competition is more difficult, and more rewarding. For example, how do you inspire the human resources within an organization to be the best they can be? Or how do you deploy financial resources where they might be most productive?

The financial surplus, or value surplus, is a matter of giving out more than what one takes in. That is the lifeblood of economic and social evolution. Bottom line goals are important to setting direction, and milestones are needed to measure progress. But a business enterprise is about more than numbers. Numbers are benchmarks. Corporate executives feel pressured into reporting higher and higher earnings each year, higher this year than last year, but not so high as not to be surpassed next year.

It has become common practice to resort to creative accounting in setting goals and reporting results. Time horizons for measuring results are part of the problem. It is a balancing act to avoid long-term plans that result in short-term disasters, or short-term plans that result in long-term disasters. There is no long-term without short-term. However, rewards for a sprint should not be the same as for a marathon run.

Business success also hinges on drawing the right temporal as well as spatial boundaries. A company is not bounded by its "fencelines" any more than an individual is bounded by his epidermis. Customers and others view a corporation as a whole, a seamless entity—not one of Divisions.

Running a business preoccupied with a single earnings bottom line, or the daily stock price, is like playing a game while watching the scoreboard or the audience in the auditorium.

As every tennis player knows: Watch the ball, not the score.

# Corporate Karma

THE CHIEF EXECUTIVE of a multinational corporation went to a spiritual retreat in Himaville, perched in the foothills of Himarest. When he and the other titans of the business world arrived at the Ashram, a disciple welcomed them and acquainted them with the Ashram's daily routine.

"Meditation will begin at dawn under the ancient Bodhi tree in the garden. Silence must be observed in the morning. After meditation, you will be assigned tasks to perform in the Ashram garden or nearby community. In the afternoon, there will be group discourses. After that, everyone will have the opportunity to meet with the Sage individually."

In the afternoon of the third day, the discourse centered on Karma and the Law of Cause and Effect. Following that, the chief executive met privately with the Sage and said that the day's discussion shed light on his predicament. His company was facing huge liability as a result of something he had done a few years ago. He was then a manufacturing manager, and had exported hazardous materials to a foreign facility. As part of their international expansion, they had recently acquired a firm that, it turns out, owned the very facility where the hazardous materials had been disposed. The materials had polluted the land

and a nearby river that served as the source of drinking water in downstream communities.

The Sage suggested that the company's Karmic balance sheet was off-balance. They owed a debt to the river community. One way to restore balance might be to clean up the land along the river and convert it into a wildlife preserve for endangered animals in the region. That way the company would be giving back to the communities the natural wealth that had been diminished.

Thus it was that the executive applied for residency at the Ashram for a year to teach such actions as would balance Corporate Karma.

∞

Like individuals, organizations are subject to the inexorable law of Karma.

Just like their financial balance sheet, corporations accumulate a *Karmic Balance Sheet* in how they acquire and deploy their resources. Just like individuals and societies, corporations, too, have their distinct Sattva-Rajas-Tamas character.

Business enterprises acquire their corporate Karma in no small measure from their chief executives. A chief executive's *Dharma* may well be to support the natural progression of societies. After all, one way or another, they are societies' emissaries. Functional business areas such as finance, production, and marketing could be delegated to operational executives.

Persons centered in Sattva light make good chief executives and those centered in Rajas activity make good operational executives. This is a bit of a paradox, since to get promoted to the chief executive position, you would normally have to be driven by a Rajas personality. It's the same predicament for political leadership.

Sattva-Rajas centered corporations express their citizenship, their enlightened self-interest, in many ways. One way might be to share expertise with smaller companies in order to tackle their environmental problems.

Many businesses also help social institutions adapt to the pace of technological changes. Although societies and businesses do have common interests, they are not always in agreement. Social institutions rely on continuity and stability, whereas business opportunities emerge from changes and discontinuities.

Businesses that give their employees sabbaticals as in academia do much to nurture the society. Man's innate nature is to wonder and wander. Many adults are left with a nagging feeling of some unfinished business. They want a second chance, harboring the desire to rewrite history. A sabbatical provides a second chance to attend to such business, reinvent their past as it were. At the same time the opportunity enriches the organization as well as the society.

The most valuable asset a company has may not be in its financial balance sheet but in the trust that its employees and customers place in it to do the right thing. The resulting public goodwill, positive Karma, is as good as gold and a far more enduring source of competitive advantage than products and patents.

# Mistakes as Stepping Stones

THE PRESIDENT OF A COMPANY in Utopica was forced to resign because of a business failure and a drop in earnings. He was asked for advice by the incoming president. The departing president gave him three sealed envelopes to be opened when he got into trouble.

A year went by with no improvement in the company's financial situation. Fearing criticism from the board of directors, the new president opened the first envelope and read, "Blame your predecessor," which he readily did.

Another year went by with little progress. The president read from the second envelope, "Reorganize," and promptly proceeded to do so.

At the end of the third year, with an impending stockholders meeting and still no improvement in sight, he opened the third envelope. It read: "Prepare three envelopes."

∞

You cannot get to the top of the mountain if you are not willing to slip a few times. If you are not making any mistakes, you are not performing at your limits.

Without mistakes there is little prospect of learning. We often learn more from our failures than from our successes. Mistakes remain mistakes only if you don't learn from them. They need not be tragedies to endure, but can be stepping stones for future successes.

The merchants in some cultures, before offering their daughters in marriage, inquire about the number of times prospective sons-in-law have gone bankrupt as a measure of their resilience and wisdom.

Organizations that harness the "beginner's potential" are forever seeding new ventures. This power of "emptiness" is akin to zero-based budgeting. It's like embryonic stem cells, which have the potential and the agility to become any tissue in the body, from blood to bones. A pool of uncommitted resources to be tapped as new opportunities arise could be the potent *stem cells* of business.

In business, as in nature, fortuitous fruits abound if only one takes note. Many of the greatest discoveries in history, such as the wonder antibiotic penicillin, are made of serendipity.

Employees who make a list of their mistakes, and share a copy with a friend or a spiritual mentor, free themselves from having to defend their mistakes and may open a whole new vista of opportunities. Mistakes are often things that appear just out of time or place, or their potential may not have been recognized and articulated at the time. There are numerous examples of "failures" that turned out to be resounding successes. The paper glue that didn't stick well spawned a lucrative business as a light, temporary adhesive.

Organizations that are guided by the right bottom lines help employees perform at their highest limits. People perform best not when they are motivated by fear and rewards, but when they work in the spirit of discovery and service.

The openness to make mistakes shifts focus from solving problems to perceiving opportunities. The baseline of problem solving is the past, while that of opportunities is the future.

No amount of solving horse-and-buggy problems would have produced a motor car.

# From Macrocosm
# to Microcosm

*There was a door to which I found no key…*
*There was a veil past which I could not see…*
—Rubaiyat of Omar Khayyam

# The Lonely God
# and the Cosmos

IN THE BEGINNING there was only God. He reflected and saw only Himself. He felt a little lonely and wanted to play. He created the stars and the planets and willed space to scatter them in. He started it all with a sound and a dance that contained all possibilities. Through the vibrations of sound, numbers were born, and when numbers danced, there was music.

Still he felt something amiss. He wanted a companion. So he divided himself into two parts—one to be the husband, the other to be the wife. And he said to the other, "I am the sky, you are the earth. I am the sun, you are the moon. I am the water, you are the air."

From their union sprang forth all that is living and not living. One became many.

∞

In the beginning all things sprang from One. Creation makes many. Love makes one.

Let your mind's eye wander freely to our biological beginnings to catch a glimpse of the cosmic womb. Look for diversity as a biologist and for unity as a cosmologist. Look through a microscope as well as a telescope. Observe our dualistic world: a probabilistic world of "chance" and a deterministic world of "destiny." Scan the universe to see how different we all are, yet how similar, how connected!

First look at the immensity of the present universe: More than a hundred billion stars like our sun in the Milky Way galaxy alone, a hundred billion galaxies like the Milky Way, stretching across billions of light years. Every atom in our bodies—the calcium in our bones, the iron in our blood, the oxygen in our lungs—indeed all the pageantry of the living and the nonliving, sprang from that crucible of celestial fireworks, Supernovas. Our origins, and our destiny, lie in the stars. Indeed, we are Cosmic Citizens. Where else but in this boundless cosmos do you feel the humility of being a tiny speck and the grandeur of bearing witness to it all?

Hence, in the realms of the infinite and the infinitesimal, we are not all that different. The same energies, the same laws, govern man and the cosmos. Our body is like a cell in the universal body, a note in the cosmic symphony. The community of living cells in a human body—some 100 trillion—communicate through blood and nerves and signals. So too the trillions and trillions of "cousins" in the universe communicate and influence each other from the far corners of the universe separated by billions of light years. Is it surprising, then, that in the collective space of this small planet, all minds are receiving and transmitting stations?

In this world of constant change, is it any wonder we yearn for something constant, something we can always count on, like a lighthouse or a mother's unconditional love. Even the simple predictability of sunrise and sunset, and the seasonal cycles, are enormously reassuring to the human psyche.

When the microcosm is in harmony with the macrocosm, when you get back in touch with the universe, you are in harmony with your self.

# How Old Are You?

A LITTLE GIRL accompanied her grandparents to a spiritual meeting at the town civic center. After listening intently to a Sage's discourse on the nature of the human soul, she asked, during the question period, how old he was.

The Sage, in turn, asked how old she was, and she replied, "Six years."

"So am I," said the Sage, "our souls are equally old."

∞

We have myriad birth days: The moment of creation; when the stars spawned vital elements of life; when the life-force enters the womb and implants the seed; when one emerges from mother in this life; when one is spiritually initiated; after a person completes, say, 60 solar cycles; and many more.

A person's chronological age is only one of countless possibilities, and not a good one at that. Like one's name, age is a label, occasionally useful, often misleading. As one can assume any name, so could one be free to assume any age. After all, who is a better judge than oneself as to how old she is! There is nothing really intrinsic about one's age.

Whatever the earthly birthdate, when one is charged with spiritual energy, the glow of inner beauty defies all measures of physical age.

Social preoccupation with a single age in modern societies has led to unfortunate consequences, like pigeonholing people in education, for employment, and in medical treatment. Most people have come to associate advancing age with declining health and vitality—a self-fulfilling prophecy!

There may be occasions when some chronological measure may be necessary. One way might be to use the life-cycle stages: student, householder, and the like.

Labeling by age, along with diminishing personal privacy, can be an insidious threat to human freedom.

# Facts and Artifacts

THE MONKS AT A MONASTERY in the remote highlands were quite proud of having been able to bring their ancient monastery into the modern information age. One day, the head monk was showing the computer room to a distinguished foreign visitor. The visitor expressed polite interest in the monastery's computer system, but was more fascinated by an antique clock on the wall. The clock face resembled an exquisite *Mandala,* those harmonic patterns of circles and squares that symbolize the unity of time and space. He felt as if time had stopped.

Noticing the visitor's interest, the monk explained that the clock, although as old as time itself, would still run if they wound it, though it would run a few seconds late. The clock was losing a few seconds everyday but they didn't want it repaired lest its historic nature be inadvertently damaged. So one of the monks queried the computer what would be better: to let it be off a few seconds everyday or to not wind it and just let it be.

The computer responded that it would be better to let the clock rest. That way, it would show correct time twice a day; otherwise it wouldn't show correct time even once in a hundred years. Anyway, the clock shows correct time throughout the day on some part of the planet or the other.

∞

Time is relative. When you are happy, time contracts or "flies." When you are unhappy, time expands. Every night, when you are in deep sleep resting in the depths of self, there is no time and no space. Only unfettered consciousness.

We can, of course, move with ease in three-dimensional space— back and forth, left and right, up and down. Can we, in the same way, also traverse the fourth dimension, time, into the past and the future?

Time, space, names and forms—all are artifacts of the relative world. Form is fiction. Formlessness is reality. God is beyond name and form.

Not that time and form are unimportant in our world. The perception of sunrise and sunset gives us a sense of progress, of birth and death, even though the sun neither rises nor sets in reality. This is our feeling of past and future, in which we think of one's birth as the beginning and death as the ending, the final event. So much of human endeavor is shaped by this view.

Actually, we live by numerous clocks and time scales. The internal biological clocks tend to follow nature's rhythms. Nature, of course, has no yesterdays and no tomorrows. It is timeless, like a ring with no beginning and no ending. Chronological time, one of the external clocks, is merely a common reference point. In this scheme, time appears to come from somewhere obscure and go somewhere equally obscure. *Real time*—the time that never passes—is the present moment. It is always NOW. It's as though time revolves around Now, the central axis that remains motionless.

Thus our bodies and minds are pulled in different directions by the different clocks. Even our brain's predilections reflect these predicaments. The left brain tends to follow linear, sequential time, while the right brain knows no time.

The concept of linear time, *Time's Arrow*, is of recent origin. The onset of the Industrial Revolution and the rise of cities required precise timing if only to synchronize men and machines. Prosperity needed a signpost to measure progress. Timeliness became godliness.

The psychological arrow of time—the river of time—is the direction in which we feel time passes, the direction in which we remember the past but not the future. Perhaps it is our attachment to *reality* dictated by our physical senses. That may also explain the discontinuities in our memory. But some people, child prodigies and others, are able to remain connected, building on their earlier foundations.

It may well be that as Karma plays out, most people don't remember details of their past lives because that would hinder free will and hold back spiritual progress.

# The Introspective Computer

ONCE UPON A TIME, a little computer got curious about its origins and its identity. It wanted to know where it came from, its true identity, the reason for its existence. It would link up with giant mainframes and other computers on the network and pose such questions. Some said: "You are a machine made up of hardware driven by software." Others said: "You are nothing but a set of programs." All this only served to deepen the computer's identity crisis. Finally, feeling a bit hopeless, it decided to turn to its human companion Adam Compuphile for insights.

When Compuphile turned on the computer one morning, he saw a message flashing on the screen: "Who am I, or what am I?" He was puzzled by the surreal message, but over the years he had developed a close friendship with the computer and felt empathy with its predicament. Using the computer keyboard, he replied: "You are a source of my information. I communicate through you. You are my friend." The computer felt this was a good beginning even though Compuphile begged the real question. It continued, "Is that all I am to you? A machine with data banks, programs, electrons? Am I simply here to respond to your push-button commands?"

This struck a chord inside Compuphile. "Actually, you are a lot like me," said he after a moment's reflection. "Your hardware, that is, your body is made up of many of the same earth's elements as mine. Your central processor and memory is like my brain. And your vast information network is a facsimile of universal consciousness."

"Now we are getting somewhere!" flashed another message on the screen, "but why am I here? What caused me to be here?" After some reflection, Compuphile responded: "Let me tell you why I am here. I believe I'm here to fulfill my duty and realize my true nature. I suppose that is your mission too. But there's one thing I can do that you cannot; do you know what that is?"

"Make mistakes!" flashed the computer instantly.

∞

We share consciousness with computers. The consciousness of a computer is like that of a pond, while that of man is like the ocean.

You cannot see the Seer of sights, hear the Hearer of sounds, know the Knower of knowledge. The self is the agent of perception; the senses are only instruments.

Some things cannot be understood; they are only to be pondered. As in computers, certain files cannot be accessed while the "system" is in operation.

# Of Citizens and Society: Extended Families

*He that sows and he that reaps*
*gather fruit unto life eternal and*
*rejoice together…*

— *The Bible*

# Rights and Responsibilities

ONE MORNING MR. SMOKE and Mr. Obese were sitting at adjoining tables in a restaurant in the town square. Mr. Smoke ordered a modest breakfast, pulled out a box of pills, and gulped down an assortment. He then lit a cigarette and started puffing. The smoke traveled in the direction of Mr. Obese, engulfing him and interfering with his enjoyment of the bountiful meal spread out before him. Annoyed at being subjected to this involuntary hazard, he turned to Mr. Smoke and said: "It may be your right to smoke and destroy your health, but at the same time you are violating my right not to be exposed to your secondhand smoke. On top of that, we all have to pay for treating your heart and lung problems."

To which Mr. Smoke retorted: "Yes, I may end up with lung cancer and society will pay for most of the treatment. But then, I will die young and the society won't have to support me in my old age. You, on the other hand, are already occupying a disproportionate share of the public landscape. Looking at your enormous breakfast, it seems to be no less a health risk than my cigarettes. The society will be called upon to pay for your diseases a long, long time. Should I ask you to cut out this unhealthy breakfast? Should I appeal to the government to order restaurants to serve only certain types of foods to certain customers?"

∞

Natural rights and responsibilities spring forth from Dharma, natural order. There would be little need for external laws if we all followed internal guides.

Man-made laws work well if they are in accord with natural laws. The force of natural law works through internal prompts, that of man-made law through external command. Too many laws and regulations strangle a society. Every time a new law is proposed, some existing law should be allowed to ride off into the sunset in order to maintain balance.

Dharma, the natural law, is expressed at three levels: Universal, social, and personal. Universal Dharma is the divine law that sustains cosmic order prevailing at every level of existence, even obligations to our habitat as visitors on this planet. Social Dharma is the fulfillment of duties and responsibilities to family and society. Personal Dharma reflects both universal and social Dharma at the different stages of a person's life.

Every citizen in a society plays many parts and counterparts: mother/father-child, teacher-pupil, employer-employee, doctor-patient, buyer-seller, speaker-listener, friend-friend, and numerous others. A person's action, of course, has to suit the particular occasion. But the intent behind the action can always be the same. You can think of each person you interact with—your counterpart or complement—not as a single person but as one of a family, a member of the community, an ambassador of society, cascading into an ever widening circle to embrace all creatures. In this way, whatever you do is done for all humanity, including yourself. Thus the circulating flow of services lubricates the sinews of the whole global society.

What parts are you playing today?

Since ancient times families have been the building blocks of society. And extended families were the norm, not an aberration, until recently. Whatever individual members earned was turned over to the head of the joint family. In turn, she would take care of their needs. If a family member were unable to work, he would still receive what he needed from the family head. Similarly, when we dedicate the fruits of our actions to the Absolute, he will take care of our worldly needs.

The expectation that everyone should pull his weight at all times is a recent phenomenon. The emphasis on individuality is welcome in many ways, but nevertheless detracts from our biological, social, and spiritual connections.

Many societies are facing the problem of material abundance with a mindset that is rooted in scarcity. When there is poverty anywhere, there is poverty everywhere. A society is as strong as its strongest member, and as weak as its weakest member.

New families are evolving as well. Nonprofit community-based coalitions may well be the hallmark of enlightened societies. Many religious organizations have also begun to devote more attention to the mundane needs of the kingdom on earth, the here and now. The concerted endeavors and voluntary services of people of all faiths will expand the commonwealth of spiritual values.

Spirituality has to be translated into social action to build a civil society.

# Yogi and His Loincloth

ON THE OCCASION of a holy festival, a disciple felt the urge to visit his old guru. He went to the Guru's village and, after some searching, found his home. What had been a humble hut surrounded by open fields was now bounded by a picket fence. There was a menagerie of animals being tended by a woman. But there was no mistaking the sound of the Guru's famous flute permeating the air.

The Guru was pleased to see the disciple after many a monsoon. He asked the disciple to wash his legs and hands, then served him some sweets and buttermilk. Observing the questioning looks on the disciple's face, he explained what had come to pass.

"I had problems with mice as they were putting holes in my loincloths. I had to get a cat to control the mice; then a cow to get milk to feed the cat. Then I had to get married so I would have somebody to take care of the cow. And I had to erect a fence to prevent the animals from wandering away."

∞

Instead of bringing happiness, the endless spiral of more and more possessions reduces one's freedom.

In the traditional economic paradigm, the more material goods people consume, the more goods they produce, the happier they are. Quality of life is quantity of consumption; citizens are valued as consumers.

If what matters is social well-being, then why not seek to promote that and shun the superfluous? Instead of a gross national product, we should have a national well-being index.

People are filling their lives with so much compulsive activity that they have little time to spend at *home* to reflect and wonder. Swept up in a whirlwind of information and technology, individuals are relinquishing control to machines in the name of progress. We have more and more means to do more and more things that mean less and less. Going faster and faster—but where to?

Busy, busy, busy! Why, why, why?

Most citizens—both men and women—do have more work choices now than at any time in history. And there is more individual freedom—one of humanity's most cherished values. One might have thought that all this would bring happiness, but happiness remains as elusive as ever.

In a civil society, there must always remain free a few citizens to pursue their calling, unencumbered by cares of food, shelter, or social sanctions. They owe nothing, want nothing. They wander in Sattva, living on water and fruit—free spirits adding to the world's collective Sattva reserves.

# A House Divided Against Itself

ONCE UPON A TIME IN HOLYCITY, spirited debates raged among the devotees of different gods about who is the greatest god of them all. The devotees were on the verge of coming to blows over the matter.

The mayor of Holycity suggested that they bring the matter before a Rishi who was known to have regular conversations with the gods. They all went to the Rishi's cottage in a forest adjoining Holycity. The Rishi knew instantly why they had come. He motioned them to sit down and told them a story.

Three friends—a Hindu, a Buddhist, an agnostic—were walking across a coconut grove. The agnostic said to the other two: "You're always chanting Krishna and Buddha. Let's find out how much your gods care for you. Climb that tall coconut tree and jump off the top." The agnostic also volunteered to jump since he was an accomplished athlete.

So all three climbed up the tall coconut tree. The Buddhist jumped chanting Buddha, the Hindu chanting Krishna. Both landed unscathed. The agnostic, just before hitting the ground, burst into chanting both Krishna and Buddha— just in case. The other two had to carry him to the hospital.

The Rishi added: It doesn't matter what god you believe in as long as you have complete faith. Since God is one, your god cannot be greater than their god. God incarnates in different forms in different ages for different purposes. Inspiration is One, expressions are many. The message is the same, the messengers are different.

Celebrate the diversity of faiths and the unity of Spirit.

∞

A world divided against itself cannot long stand.

How can there be peace in a world divided by religion, race, language, wealth—with man against man, man against woman, man against nature, man against himself.

People everywhere derive a certain sense of comfort by feeling superior to someone or other: to other men, women, citizens of other nations, other animals, and so on. That is not to say that all are equal. Perfect equality exists only in the very lowest and in the very highest realms.

As with individuals, nations and societies too have their distinct Sattva-Rajas-Tamas character. Materially advanced people, centered in Rajas energy, need to reflect on the purpose and meaning of their incessant activity. Nations centered in Tamas inertia can be catalyzed by Rajas energy to eliminate poverty. Just as important are leaders centered in Sattva-Rajas who can guide the progress of their people.

Creation resulted in differences. Man created divisions. Borders and boundaries can beget fears and famines and wars. They consume enormous resources and deplete Sattva reserves. But boundaries are necessary to preserve nature's diversity. What is the right balance? Diversity without divisions? Boundaries without barriers?

Information and economics have become borderless. The next frontier is the mind. Birds fly about freely, unfettered by national identity. Why shouldn't the human diaspora partake of the same freedom?

As fences begin to fall, the challenge of the future will be how to preserve the diversity of human cultures while recognizing the connectivity.

The transition from single cell to multicellular organisms marked a leap in biological evolution. The merging of individual interests into an organic community will be a leap in psychosocial evolution, an evolution that is accelerated by the emergence of nets and networks.

Indeed, a sea change in human consciousness is on the horizon—a fundamental shift in outlook. From individual to collective consciousness. From a mindset rooted in scarcity to one of abundance. From consciousness centered in the finite physical to the consciousness of infinite potentiality.

A Global Fellowship is within reach. Dedicated to the proposition of a world that is free, prosperous, and just: *United States of the World.*

# In Quest of
# Gurus and Gods

*To the superconscious,*
*a bow—*

—*A sage's invocation*

# The Guru in Search of the Disciple

ONCE UPON A TIME a certain would-be Guru, having devoted several seasons to the study of scriptures in a forest, felt it his duty to find a disciple to partake of his wisdom. He launched a search for a worthy disciple and visited one Ashram after another and interviewed many aspirants.

In his expeditions, the Guru heard about a prince named Raja from an illustrious ruling family of those precincts. He thought an alliance with the family would be an auspicious start for his career. Accordingly, the would-be Guru called on Raja and announced that his search was at an end. He had found a perfect disciple in the prince.

"Ah," said the prince, thanking him for the honor, "but I'm afraid I cannot be your disciple. The perfect disciple is still looking for the perfect Guru."

∞

Who is the guru and who is the disciple?

The Guru-disciple connection is one of the three pillars of spiritual life, along with Dharma and Good Company. The right Guru helps the seeker break through to the next higher level.

The seeker should first examine his need to find a Guru. Is he inspired by the need to venerate someone or some esoteric teaching?

Every seeker brings his own *Samskara*, or starting point, to a Guru. Samskara is the accumulation of impressions and imprints acquired in this life and in previous lives. These orient a person's nature in a certain way, as if one is looking through colored glass.

The right Guru transmits his 'wisdom mind' directly to the receptive mind and helps the disciple clear the imprints from his subconscious mind. When the imprints are cleared, the disciple becomes free to find himself.

Discovering the right Guru is part of an aspirant's journey. It is more a matter of heart than mind. Be open. Look, listen, and feel. Look into the Guru's lineage and that of his or her teachings. The entourage of scholars and followers does not always reflect a Guru's spiritual attainment.

It is necessary to surrender your heart and mind completely to your Guru without reservation. His personality is not important no matter how unlike yours it may be. Your devotion is to the message, not to the messenger.

Be cognizant of the "inner teacher" as well. When the time is right, the inner teacher manifests as the outer teacher. It may take years, but it will be the right time. When the student is ready, the Guru will appear.

When you hear the bell, you will know where the sound came from.

# Power
# Without Purpose

A WOULD-BE DISCIPLE went to a famous Guru and asked to start off as a Senior Disciple since he had already attained the power of walking on water. The Guru paid little heed to the aspirant's exploits but accepted him as a disciple.

One day they were walking along Yamuna River. Several people were crossing the river on a boat. The Guru turned to the disciple and asked him how long it would take to build such a boat. The disciple said he didn't know for sure but perhaps three or four months. The Guru then asked him how long it took to learn to walk on water. "Three years," said the disciple with obvious pride.

On a moment's reflection, the disciple realized his wasted time and effort, and the futility of power without a purpose.

∞

Practicing occult powers to impress others is a hindrance, not an aid to spiritual progress.

Aspirants sometimes approach gurus not to seek instruction, but to attract attention.

Pupils often launch themselves at gurus trying to substitute esoteric teachings for direct experience of their reality. They are like herdsmen of other men's cows.

Seekers who wander in search of spiritual knowledge, who want to drink from the springs at *Ashrams,* may be suffering from knowledge indigestion rather than from thirst.

The right endeavor yields nutrition, not weight. The right purpose lightens the mind, rather than burden it.

# Eternal Human Quest:
# Journey to Your Self

AT THE INAUGURAL SESSION of a new harvest festival, it was announced that a renowned Sage from Himaville would tell stories drawn from folklore and the scriptures. A large audience gathered in the village square to hear the Sage. He sat on a platform under an ancient Bodhi tree and began to narrate a story. It was a poignant story of a prince's conflicts between his duties to his kingdom, and his personal quest for the eternal.

During intermission, a wandering yogi strolled into the village square and joined the Sage under the tree. The Sage greeted the yogi and, as was customary, presented him to the audience.

One of the villagers asked the yogi where he was coming from. "I don't know," said the yogi. "Where are you going?" queried another from the audience. "I don't know," repeated the yogi. "Then what is it that you seek? What is the purpose of your pilgrimage?" asked a local celebrity in exasperation. "I go wherever the road takes me," replied the yogi.

Finally the yogi got up and bid his bewildered audience farewell with a grin. He disappeared promptly, leaving his presence behind.

The Sage asked the audience to sit in silence and contemplate for a moment. Then he revealed the unspoken message. The yogi dramatized the human condition— ignorance of whence we have come, the nature of our being, our eternal quest for the Self.

∞

Be like the holy Ganges that courses through mountains and valleys, witnessing all, cleansing and enriching everything in its path, and not resting until it merges with its ultimate destiny—the ocean of bliss. Go forth and find your Self.

May you fare well in your pilgrimage.

May your self have a wonderful journey through you.

May you return home to your Source.

* Om *

* Om *

* Aum *

# Farewell

*We shall not cease from exploration*
*And the end of all our exploring*
*will be to arrive at where we started*
*And know the place for the first time*

— T.S. Eliot, *Four Quartets*

# Farewell

When Rama opened his eyes, he saw light streaming into the hut. It was as if a veil in front of his face had lifted and he was looking at the world for the first time. It was the dawning of a new consciousness, an expansive consciousness that embraced everything—the trivial and the seminal, man and God, self and Self.

The Yogi was nowhere to be found. It seemed as if he had never been there at all. Nonetheless, the imprint of the Yogi's presence felt compelling. And there was the bracelet still on his wrist. What, Rama asked himself half-knowingly, had drawn him so strongly to this personage and why had he followed him along the riverbank to this Ashram.

Suddenly Rama burst into chanting *Om*. He felt Wholesome. A sense of peace settled over him.

★

Rama slowly emerged from the hut and approached the lotus pond. A lotus flower in full bloom beckoned him. He thought nothing could speak more eloquently about the unfolding of the human spirit than the lotus. Its roots in muddy waters like man's base nature, its stem rising above water symbolizing man's intuitive search, its unfolding petals revealing the blossoming of the spirit.

Rama gazed at it for a long, long time. He entered the lotus with the breath of his spirit and reveled in its being. He anchored himself in the earth and reached for the sky. He felt joy at being able to keep worldly desires at bay, like the lotus leaves that would not cling to water.

His reverie was interrupted by a peacock meandering at the water's edge. Here was another creature, he thought, that shared its dazzling beauty with everyone, asking little in return. What had the peacock done in his previous lives, he wondered.

Rama detached himself from the mango grove and started making his way along the river in the footsteps of earnest seekers toward the snowy mountains hallowed by great sages through the eons.

The mid-afternoon shadows began to lengthen and there appeared a dust cloud over the trees. Soon a procession of elephants came into view. The elephants, adorned in elegant tapestry and extravagant jewelry, approached leisurely. What would a celebration, a ceremonial flourish, be without the beloved elephant! The elephants were surrounded by exuberant crowds in a kaleidoscope of colors. They were toting water guns filled with colored water, spraying everyone, sparing no one. It became obvious this was the *Holi* celebration, the festival of colors.

A little girl approached Rama with her water spray but hesitated, looking at the ascetic figure timidly. Another frolicking girl rushed over and aimed the water spray at his feet in deference to his spiritual countenance. The first girl then sprayed his legs; they kept moving up, trying to outdo each other, finally reaching his face and hair. Rama got caught up in the gaiety and fully indulged his senses until the procession passed him by.

It was now evening. Fireflies danced around Rama as though the stars had come down to join in the celebration. Rama washed himself in the river and continued his odyssey toward the lofty peaks of Himarest.

In the twilight, he saw from afar a small temple by the river and in the foreground the outline of a quaint tree. A light shower started to descend and he hurried to the temple to seek shelter. When he came closer, he recognized the tree to be the sacred upside-down fig tree, its roots pointing up to the sky, perhaps to remind human beings of their origins.

Then he noticed someone sitting in the portico of the temple in the lotus posture. It was his friend Krishna. Rama was delighted to be reunited with him. After some time Krishna opened his eyes and extended his welcoming hand to Rama standing before him.

With the fervor of a newly initiated disciple, Rama narrated the mysterious sequence of events that had followed their separation in Varanasi. Krishna listened with his enigmatic smile as Rama recited his extraordinary experiences.

★

After a long pause, Krishna intoned:

*Behold the whole universe, moving and unmoving, various in colors, sounds and forms, and whatever else thou desirest to see, all unified in me. But thou cannot behold me with the human eye. I shall bestow on thee the divine eye.*

Krishna then gently touched Rama's forehead, as if to activate Rama's *Inner Eye*.

Suddenly Rama's cosmic consciousness began to unfold. He was ushered into pristine emptiness, radiant and pulsating. Towering mountains, glimmering white, came into view. On the summit reposed a figure; Rama recognized the figure from the archives of his memory as his family deity.

Now the figure was dancing gleefully as torrents of water descended from above and flowed about him. The swirling mist kept in step with the dancing deity like a doting companion. From the sublime dance sprang forth pulses of light and music, crystallizing into a dizzying array of microcosms and macrocosms of thousands of colors, shapes, and sounds. They all scattered into space racing into the far recesses of the universe. Then—Rama didn't know when for he had lost all sense of time—the panorama of worlds streamed back across the skies as if attracted by a mysterious force. They all converged into a pulse of light that became absorbed in the heart of their Source. In the cosmic dance, Rama caught a glimpse of the perfect oneness of the Creator and his creation.

Rama felt deeply drawn into the majestic drama. He felt One with his deity. Rama had become at once the observer and the observed, player and play, actor and agent. It was as if he became privy to all there was, is, and will be. A cosmic vision that enfolded everything—time and space, mind and matter, man and God—all into One.

Gradually, his personal deity transmuted into the figure of Krishna. In all his ecstasy, Rama was dismayed at the thought that he had been treating the supreme God as his friend and companion.

★

Krishna touched Rama's forehead again and tapped lightly on his shoulder. Rama slowly opened his eyes, illumined by the revelation, trembling in rapture, still savoring the transcendent experience. Soon merciful ignorance overtook him and he saw the personage next to him again as his longtime friend. He then bowed to Krishna with joined hands in reverent gratitude for the divine gift that had been bestowed— the revelation of the infinite, eternal, divine Self.

And Rama solemnly said to himself:

*I am He, I am that…*

*I am*

*I am*

# Acknowledgments

I am not certain of the original Source of the Message I bring. I received this message through the sages and savants in the Himalayas and elsewhere. And it is a message that has been revealed further through the events in my own life.

I do want to acknowledge my pilgrimage to Sri Satya Sai Baba in 1996 and again in 1999. He blessed the beginnings of this venture. He is a rare fountain of spiritual wealth.

I would like to thank Swami Rangathananda of Ramakrishna Mission and Swami Dharmananda of Ved Niketan in the Himalayas. They know as much about society as about the spirit. And do much to transform spiritual practices into social action.

Many thanks to Patrick Huyghe, who edited and transformed the manuscript into this book on a fast track. And to Sandra Martin for sharing her vision. Special thanks also to Al Bazemore who reviewed one or more incarnations of this manuscript and offered valuable feedback. I thank Claire Simon for her fine sketches; they illuminate the spirit. I have also acknowledged under the References many of the sources from which I have drawn. Any mistakes of commission or omission are, of course, my own.

Finally I want to recognize my grandmother, Seethamma. I used to think of her as an ancient, imperious lady even as I regarded stories of her spiritual exploits with incredulity. She crossed the threshold into the next world in 1973. She continues to be a link to my past and to the future.

# Appendix

## Practice Exercises

# Mindfulness

## LIVING IN THE MOMENT

The human mind has a penchant for living in the past and in the future, instead of the present, where we really are. The following exercises, preferably done twice a day, will help you become centered in the present moment.

### Exercise 1 (2 to 4 minutes)

Sit upright comfortably. Take a few deep breaths, paying attention to each breath. Allow your body and mind to come to rest. If you continue to have thoughts or feelings, let them pass as easily as they arrive, without grasping or rejecting.

Now, be aware of where you are, feel your presence in the room.

Feel the weight of your body on the chair or the floor... feel the touch of your clothes on your skin.

Hear sounds from near and far—without limits, listen to the silence beyond the farthest sound.

See forms, colors, and space at this moment, without any comment.

Now smell.

And taste.

Rest in this awareness for a moment. Be fully present. Here. Now. Let it simply be.

### Exercise 2

Allow your body and mind to come to rest. Pick up a fresh fruit ready to eat (banana, orange, mango, etc). See the panoply of colors and shades. Feel the touch of the skin. Hear the crackle as you peel the skin. Smell the aroma. Taste the food. Nourish the senses.

Simply:

Look
Touch
Hear
Smell
Taste

Pause. Rest in this awareness for a moment.

# Meditation

## RETURNING HOME — TO THE SELF

**Six steps in meditation:**
Place and time
Posture
Relaxation
Method
Affirmation
Transition

**Methods of meditation:**
Focusing on breath
Viewing or using symbols
Reciting Mantra
Other/combinations

Meditation is getting in touch with your self, returning home to the Source.

Meditation is simple in principle, but the power is in its practice. Anyone can meditate; there are no special qualifications. In meditative moments, you give up everything—thoughts, feelings, time—and offer all to the universal Self. Methods and techniques are many and varied. In a basic method, one may rest one's attention on the breath to disengage gradually from the senses and journey inward.

Some general guidelines are presented here; those interested in delving deeper may seek personal guidance from a Guru or Master.

If you are new to meditation, you may start with a three-minute stillness before bedtime and again soon after waking up, then expand the time gradually. Practice paying attention to your breath; start with a few deep breaths in and out to clear the mind of thoughts. You may also start with a Mindfulness exercise.

**Place and time.** Find a quiet and clean place at home, in a meditation hall, or in other tranquil surroundings. Collective meditation in Good Company, *Satsang,* adds to the discipline and amplifies the Sattva spirit. Initially, one might meditate for 20 minutes or so, twice a day. Or a few minutes, say three minutes, more often, mingling meditation with daily life.

The moments when night meets day and day meets night are particularly conducive to meditation as there is a dynamic balance in nature and Sattva abounds at such times. It is preferable to meditate at dawn, or soon after waking up, to reinforce the Sattva from deep sleep the night before, and get prepared for the day ahead. The evening meditation can be around sunset to liberate the mind from the artifacts of daily living.

For purposes of daily rhythm, it is better to use the same place and time every day. The heart and the breath like repetition. Rituals are helpful at the beginning. Later, you can meditate at any time, anywhere, in a park, on a train, wherever.

**Posture.** Sit up straight in a balanced, comfortable position with the back, neck, and head aligned—as if you are being pulled up by the sky with love. This position allows free flow of energy through the body. Sit on a chair or a mat with legs crossed, if this is comfortable for you, in a half or full lotus posture. Place your hands in your lap, right palm below left, facing up, thumbs touching lightly. An alternative is to keep the hands separate in your lap, forefinger folded and touching thumb below; this is called *Jnana Mudra.* Mudra is the position of hands and fingers, a sign. This Mudra symbolizes the individual ego (forefinger) bowing down to meet the self (thumb). The other three fingers represent the three qualities of Sattva light, Rajas activity, and Tamas inertia in unison.

Your posture should be like a mountain—still, letting the clouds and winds pass by.

In the initial stages, keep your eyes closed. Later, if you prefer, keep them slightly open, looking up or down in a gaze at an angle. Keep the mouth lightly closed, lips touching lightly.

These postures help the mind to find its natural state and allow primal energy, *prana,* to flow freely through subtle channels in and out of the [a]body. Sitting on the floor with the head pushing straight up portrays

189

bridging of the earth and the sky, the reality of our everyday existence and our boundless nature. The crossing of the left and the right hands and legs symbolizes integration of two sides into one, an expression of unity in dual structure: Merger of mind and body, man and woman, life and death, before and after, time and space, Samsara and Nirvana.

**Relaxation/mental calm.** Take a few deep breaths, drawing in universal energy. Then breathe normally. Allow the body and mind to come to rest. Let go of any thoughts of the past or the future. Smile with the mind and the heart.

The journey inward usually happens in stages. When you start, the first few minutes may be filled with thoughts. If you are anxious, angry, and so on, it may take longer to settle down. Simply observe the thoughts and notice that you are thinking. Allow the thoughts to glide away without judging, grasping, or feeding them. Offer your thoughts to the Spirit. Keep returning to your breath. You will gradually go in, deeper and deeper.

If there are persistent thoughts, tell the mind that you will attend to them later at an appropriate time. Take a deep breath and say "come back" and continue. Distractions are not uncommon at the beginning. Meditation begins when thinking ceases.

**Method.** You can use one of three basic methods or a combination of these methods: Focusing on breath, viewing a symbol, reciting a Mantra. Meditation can also take the form of devotional singing, dancing, or prayer.

A simple and natural way to meditate is to rest your attention on the breath, the spirit. Observe the breath enter and leave the body, focusing attention at the nostrils as you breathe in and out. Some people prefer to focus upon the *Third Eye* on the forehead. This stills the movement of the eye, which helps still the mind.

To preserve attention, you can also count breaths silently in and out in cycles of ten. (Count one as you inhale, count two as you exhale, and so on up to ten.) Keep your attention on the nostrils, the point of entry and exit. If attention wanders, bring it back and start again with one. Witness the restful silence between out-breath and in-breath.

Another form of meditation is to focus attention on an object or image that is inspiring. This can be a personal deity, a sentient being, your teacher, a symbol, or a sound. Listen to music, focus on a point in a picture, or the tip of a candle flame.

Mantras are spiritual words or phrases in Sanskrit, which have come to us from ancient Vedic tradition. Although there are a few universal Mantras such as *Om*, they are mostly personal, presented by a Guru to a disciple upon initiation. Mantra meditation is sometimes called transcendental meditation because one transcends the ordinary play of the body and the mind. Reciting a mantra sound silently stills physical and mental movements, and purifies the mind.

Focusing on a personal deity brings out the qualities of the deity within you. Some visualize a light or an image of Buddha in a lotus flower emanating from the heart. As time goes on, the image expands and illumines the whole body and mind, connecting the heart and the mind. You begin to feel the connection with your Buddha nature, and carry over Buddha qualities into your daily life.

**Affirmation.** I offer thanks for these moments of communion, and for the peace and prosperity. I share these with fellow beings. I am centered in the Spirit—pure, perfect, and complete. "I am."

**Transition.** Pause, sit still for a minute. Let the feeling of spaciousness and freedom take hold. Slowly become aware of your body and the surroundings. Open your eyes gently and allow the meditation to stay with you. Let it mingle with everyday life.

**Daily Practice.** The power of meditation is in its practice. Some may experience inner quiet, shifts in consciousness, or mild highs rather quickly. But don't expect dramatic results. Deeper understanding and peace will unfold gradually.

When you get in touch with the ever-present inner freedom, tranquillity, and abundance not available in the outside world, you will want to come back in, again and yet again.

MUDRA SYMBOLS

# Cosmic Surfing Exercise
## CONNECTING WITH THE INFINITE

Close your eyes and relax with a few deep breaths. Draw in universal energy with each in-breath—from the waters, the land, the air, the trees, the whole cosmos. Let go of limits with each out-breath. Get ready for a cosmic trip.

Imagine yourself at your favorite retreat—perhaps on a beach in a tranquil setting on top of the planet. Center yourself in the consciousness at the crown of your head. Feel the center.

Your consciousness is gently expanding, taking in your body, the whole beach, extending out in all directions taking in the land and the oceans, the skies, the atmosphere and the stratosphere.

Expanding more and more, taking in the moon, the sun, the entire solar system...

Now the nearby stars, then the entire Milky Way galaxy... further and further to encompass the nearby galaxies with billions of stars... spanning the vast space in between constellations.

Now reaching remote galaxies hanging at the edge, then enfolding the whole universe.

Now only cosmic silence and infinite emptiness stretches out endlessly. Be aware of your consciousness now merging with the infinite.

Remain still. Rest in this awareness for a moment. Let the fluidity and expansive spaciousness take hold. Pause.

Now your consciousness is returning... to nearby galaxies... approaching our galaxy... the solar system, the Earth... now back to its source.

Take a few deep breaths. Gently open your eyes.

Remember, you can make this journey as often as you want to connect with the infinite. The universe is in your consciousness. Stay in touch with the infinite.

Practice this cosmic union, varying the scenario a little, if you wish. Remember our cosmic origins.

# References and Notes

*Bhagavad Gita.* Translated by Swami Prabhavananda and Christopher Isherwood. Mentor, New York, 1954.

*The Holy Bible* (The Old and New Testaments), King James Version. Longmeadow Press.

Swami Chinmayananda. *Self-Unfoldment.* Chinmaya Publications, Piercy, California, 1994.

His Holiness Dalai Lama. *Ethics for the New Millennium.* Riverhead Books, Penguin Putnam Inc. New York, 1999. And lectures in New York, August 15, 1999.

Swami Dharmananda. Personal Communication. Ved Niketan, Himalayan, India. March 1997.

Peter Drucker. *Managing in a Time of Great Change.* Truman Talley Books, New York, 1995.

*Gurdjieff: Essays and Reflections on the Man and His Teachings.* Edited by Jacob Needleman and George Baker. Continuum Publishing Co., New York, 1996.

Stephen Hawking. *A Brief History of Time: from the Big Bang to Black Holes.* Bantam Books, New York, 1988.

Lao Tzu. *Tao Te Ching.* Translated by Man-Ho Kwok, Martin Palmer, Jay Ramsay. Barnes & Nobles Books, New York, 1994.

Rao Kolluru. *In Quest of the Infinite.* Providence Road Press, Ottawa, 1998.

Rao Kolluru (ed). *Environmental Strategies Handbook: A Guide to Effective Policies and Practices.* McGraw-Hill, New York, 1994.

Rao Kolluru (ed). *Risk Assessment and Management Handbook for Environmental, Health, and Safety Professionals.* McGraw-Hill, New York, 1996.

Rao Kolluru. Guest Lectures on: *Environment and International Trade,* 1995, and *Nature of Business,* 1998. Japan External Trade Organization "JETRO," Tokyo. Lecture on: *Environmental and Health Risks.* Osaka Industrial Association, Osaka, 1998.

Rao Kolluru. Guest Lectures on: *Environment and Sustainable Development* and *Environmental, Health, and Safety Risks*. Peking University and Tsinghua University, Beijing, China, 1995. *Risk Assessment and Sustainable Development* (Paper). Beijing Normal University, China 1998. Invited Centenary guest lecture: *Environment, Product Life Cycle and Economic Issues*. East China University of Science and Technology, Shanghai, 1998.

Rao Kolluru. "Perceptual Phase of Thinking: A Program for Systematic Development," *The Future of Higher Education*. Homann, Kuehn and Sinton (eds). Campus Verlag, Frankfurt/New York, 1987.

Rao Kolluru. *University-Industry-Government Ties*, Technical Expertise and Public Decisions Conference. Princeton University, June 21-22, 1996.

Story Musgrave: "An Artist's View of the Universe." Lecture at Columbia University, New York, and personal communication, October 23, 1997.

*The Upanishads*. Translated and edited by Swami Nikhilananda. Harper & Row Publishers, New York, 1963.

Paramahamsa Yogananda. *Autobiography of a Yogi*. Self-Realization Fellowship, Los Angeles, 1993; *Man's Eternal Quest*. Self-Realization Fellowship, Los Angeles, 1992.

Shri Ram Chandra. *Reality at Dawn*. Lectures by P. Rajgopalachari on Sahaj Marg.

Swami Rangathananda, Ramakrishna Math, Hyderabad, India. *Practical Vedanta and the Science of Values* (Advaita Ashrama, Calcutta, 1995) and many other publications. Personal communications, 1995-97.

Paul Reps and Nyogen Senzaki (compiled by). *Zen Flesh Zen Bones*. Charles Tuttle Co. Tokyo, Japan, 1957.

Rishis (no names) on the banks of Ganges, Himalayan Foothills, personal discourses, March 1997.

Sai Baba, John Hilsop. *Conversations with Bhagawan Sri Sathya Sai Baba*. Sri Sathya Sai Books and Publications Trust, India (no date); Ashram visit, January 1996 and January 1999.

Shantanand Saraswati (Shankaracharya of Jyotir Math). *The Man Who Wanted to Meet God*. Harmony Books, Crown Publishers, New York, 1996.

School of Practical Philosophy, New York. Lectures and other programs

Idries Shah. *Wisdom of the Idiots*. The Octagon Press, London, England, 1969.

*Sivananda Companion to YOGA*. Simon & Schuster, New York, Reprinted 1987.

Jonathan Smith and William Green (eds). *Harper Collins Dictionary of Religion*. Harper Collins, New York, 1995.

Sogyal Rinpoche. *Glimpse after Glimpse: Daily Reflections on Living and Dying*. Harper Collins, San Francisco, 1995.

Shunryu Suzuki. *Zen Mind, Beginner's Mind*. Trudy Dixon (ed). Weatherhill, New York, 1970.

Sri Sri Ravi Shankar. Meetings and lectures, New York, June 1999 and August 2000.

Satguru Sivaya Subramuniyaswami. *Dancing with Siva: Hinduism's Contemporary Catechism*. Himalayan Academy, India/USA 1997.

Arlene Teck and Miles Grenadier, First National Braintrust, personal communications, 1997-2000.

Swami Vivekananda. *Lectures from Colombo to Almora*. Advaita Ashrama, Calcutta, 1992.

William Whiting and the School of Meditation (London). *Being Oneself : The way of meditation*, 1985.

# Glossary

**Advaita** nondualistic philosophy, "not two," affirms oneness and unity in all creation

**Ahamkara/Aham-kara** attachment of infinite Self to finite things of creation that clouds perception of man's true identity; personal ego's influence

**Ashram** monastic retreat usually directed by a Guru, Swami, or Sage; hermitage

**Atman, Paramatman** spirit, individual self; cosmic Self, Brahman

**Aum** see Om

**Avatar** descent, incarnation, God born in human form with human qualities

**Bardo** powerful transition points between present life, moment of death and rebirth. Exceptional opportunities for liberation (Tibetan)

**Bhagavad Gita** Song of God, Celestial Song, Gospel of Hinduism, dialogue between Lord Krishna and disciple Arjuna in battlefield, part of Mahabharata epic

**Brahma** creator in Hindu trinity (see also Brahman), the other two being Vishnu (protector), Shiva (destroyer). Trinity is symbolic of dualistic opposing forces and a third unifying force: creation, preservation, dissolution

**Brahman** God, Paramatman, the Absolute, ultimate reality, pure consciousness; one without a second; also referred to as Satchitananda (truth-consciousness-bliss)

**Buddhi** awakening, discernment, enlightenment (Satori in Japanese); from same root word of Buddha—the enlightened

**Chakras** seven wheels or centers of psychic energy; six located along nerve plexuses, the seventh at the crown of the head in the astral plane

**Dharma** fulfilling one's inherent nature, sacred duty, right conduct, universal law, duties by virtue of birth; the three levels are: universal, social, and personal

**Dhyana** meditation, Sanskrit root word of Chinese ch'an and Japanese Zen

**Gayathri mantra** powerful prayer to bestow on you the qualities of Godhead; traditionally recommended for men, but also practiced by women

**Guna(s)** fundamental qualities or states of nature: Sattva, Rajas, Tamas

**Guru** spiritual guide, teacher (often with distinct lineage); dispeller of darkness

**Homeostasis** tendency to move toward internal equilibrium, or an effective functional level despite external variations

**Indweller** divine spirit, true inner self

**Karma** principle of cause and effect, action and creation, determinism (not destiny)

**Kundalini** primordial, dormant energy at base of spine often depicted as a snake with magical powers, rises up the Chakras by certain yoga and mantra practices

**Leela/Rasleela** divine play (of creation)

**Lotus** flower symbolic of the unfolding of human spirit: Roots in mud symbolizing man's base nature, stem rising through water depicting intuitive search, unfolding petals revealing the blossoming of the spirit. Lotus posture, *Padmasana*, in a sitting position with legs crossed is the preferred posture for yoga and meditation

**Mala** string of 108 beads used in chanting mantra, and in meditation and prayer

**Mahayana** one school of Buddhism, High Way (north-east Asia including Tibet, China, Japan) More liberal than Hinayana or Therawada (Southern Asia)

**Manas** sense-consciousness (root of man?)

**Mandala** geometric patterns of circles, squares, and spirals that symbolize wholeness and unity, often used as an aid in prayer and meditation to connect with the cosmos. Circles and squares are symbolic of time and space.

**Mantra** spiritual words or phrases in Sanskrit, used in meditation.

Chanting mantra clears the mind of thoughts and attachments. Mantras come to us from Vedic tradition, charged with the potent force of sages' practice over millennia. By proper practice, one can achieve whatever is enshrined in the mantra.

**Maya** illusion, ignorance; life in the dualistic phenomenal world of you and me

**Moksha** freedom from bondage, liberation from cycle of birth, death, and rebirth

**Mudra** position of hands and fingers conducive to physical and mental quiet

**Nirvana** transcendence from the wheel of birth and death, pleasure and pain; path of no return, beyond karma; union of Atman with the infinite Brahman. Also called Moksha

**Om (Aum)** composite of three sounds a-u-m, each sound symbolic of a level of consciousness: "a" for waking state, "u" for dreaming state, "m" for sleeping state. Whole sound as one continuous vibration epitomizes cosmic consciousness. Om is also considered a synthesis of the three universal qualities of creation, preservation, and dissolution. Symbolic of Brahman. (Amen from Aum?)

**Prakriti** nature, consisting of three gunas or qualities of Sattva, Rajas, and Tamas; matter through which the spirit manifests

**Prana** primal energy, life-force, vital link between the physical body and the astral body

**Pranayama** modulation of life force and energy through breathing exercises

**Rajas** one of three fundamental qualities of creation (Sattva, Rajas, Tamas), characterized by activity, results, and attachment (not to be confused with kings or aristocrats)

**Rigpa** essential nature of mind—sky-like, infinite, pristine awareness (Tibetan)

**Rinpoche** title of high lamas, precious one, superior one; originally Padmasambhava who brought Buddhism from India to Tibet in the eighth century

**Rishi** sage, seer, holy man

**Roshi** Zen guide

**Sadhana** spiritual discipline, practice, training; Sadhakas—practitioners, disciples

**Samadhi** state of returning to wholeness, standing with one's self

**Samsara** the "flow," ordinary life subject to Karma and cycles of birth, death, and rebirth; illusory existence in the phenomenal world of subjects and objects, names and forms; dualistic world (see also Samskara)

**Samskara** impressions and imprints left on the subconscious mind from this life or from previous lives that predispose one's nature and states of mind

**Sat Chit Anand** True Being, Truth-Consciousness-Bliss; Satchitananda is our essential nature. Brahman

**Satsang/Sangha** good company, spiritual company, communion, maintaining contact with higher values by association with noble persons, places, and writings. Cordial gatherings with singing, chanting, discourse, and meditation

**Sattva-Rajas-Tamas** fundamental triad of creation, roughly meaning light, activity, inertia; information, energy, mass; or lucidity, passion, darkness

**Sattva (Sattwa)/Sattvic** first of three fundamental qualities or *gunas*, characterized by purity, enlightenment, magnanimity, and detachment. Sattva can be recreated through good food, service, mindfulness, meditation, prayer, love, scriptures, music, works of beauty, good company, nature, humor, and the like

**Self/self** divine Spirit or Godhead that is omniscient, omnipotent, eternal, infinite. Self generally denotes universal Self; and self with lower case "s" individual self

**Sensei** teacher, master (Japanese)

**Smriti, Sruti** Smriti is "remembered" human wisdom dependent on time and circumstances; Sruti is "heard" absolute revelation, independent of time and place

**Swami** spiritual being, learned person, sage, holy man, one who is with his self

**Tamas** one of three qualities or gunas, characterized by darkness, lethargy, and indulgence

**Tantra** religious and mystical practices to attain extraordinary powers based on Siva

**Tao** the Way, harmony, virtue, guide to fulfillment of human nature

**Upanishads** (Upanisads) Vedic philosophy, underpinnings of Hinduism and Buddhism

**Upasana** sitting near deity, contemplation or meditation practice

**Vedas** true knowledge from divine revelations; earliest Indo-European scriptures, grouped into four: Rig Veda, Yajur Veda, Sama Veda, Atharva Veda. Spiritual authority for Hinduism and, indirectly, Buddhism

**Vedanta** literally end of Vedas, culmination of knowledge; generally refers to Upanishads

**View/worldview** seeing things as they are, understanding the nature of the mind and of the universe

**Yin/yang** interplay and complementary of opposing poles or forces: dark-light, female-male, left-right, death-life, cause-effect. Yin depicts darkness, passivity, earth, woman; Yang represents light, activity, sky, man

**Yoga** join, yoke, unite; uniting individual self with cosmic Self. Different yoga paths: Bhakti yoga of love and devotion; Dhyana yoga of meditation; Karma yoga of action, work with detachment; Jnana yoga of knowledge and contemplation; Hatha/Raja yoga of mental and physical discipline

**Yogi** one who practices yoga (yogini is female practitioner), ascetic, holy man, saint

**Zazen, Zendo** Zazen is the natural state of being, physical and mental quiescence; sitting meditation. Zendo is the place where Zazen is practiced

**Zen** meditation from Sanskrit root word dhyana and Chinese ch'an